FAMILY PUZZLES

A Private Life Made Public

by Award-Winning Boston Globe Columnist

Linda Weltner

Innisfree
Press, Inc.

*A call to the
deep heart's core*

Innisfree Press, Inc.
136 Roumfort Road
Philadelphia, PA 19119-1632

Cover design by Hugh Duffy.
Cover photograph by Julie Weltner Anderson.

Library of Congress Cataloging-in-Publication Data
Weltner, Linda R., date.
    Family puzzles : a private life made public / Linda Weltner.
        p.   cm.
    ISBN 1-880913-23-2
    1. Weltner, Linda R., date—Family.   2. Women authors,
American—20th century—Family relationships.   3. Women
journalists—Massachusetts—Boston—Family relationships.
I. Title.
PS3573.E4965Z467   1998
813'.54—dc21   98-6162
    [B]   CIP

To my sister, Susan, and my brother, Ken,

my kin, my clan, my destiny,

for your willingness again and again to unravel with me

the tangled skein of our love.

"The vicarious experience that reading or listening provides

can shape our essence, change us, just as firsthand experience can.

Experience seems to be as transfusable as blood . . ."

— Sidney Jourard, *The Transparent Self*

Contents

Introduction

I became a columnist entirely by chance.

Walking along a beach in Marblehead, I came across an editor I'd worked for at a local newspaper. She was with a friend who'd been put in charge of establishing an "At Home" section in the *Boston Globe*. We chatted long enough for me to find out that several New England writers had been asked to submit essays for a column to be called "Ever So Humble." On the spot my former editor suggested I be given a chance to compete. I went home that summer afternoon feeling I had just stumbled into a momentous opportunity.

I spent two days writing my first column, another two completing the second. Late in the week, I gathered my friends together to critique what I'd written, and after a night of rewriting, I drove to the paper. A security guard phoned up to announce my arrival. I stood there stunned as word came back: The woman had never heard of me. I was tempted to run for the door, but I couldn't bear the thought of telling my friends what a coward I'd been. I left the essays behind and drove home, tears of humiliation in my eyes.

When I learned a month later that I'd been selected, I faced another crisis of confidence: I wasn't sure I could pull it off. For six months I had trouble eating, sleeping, even breathing deeply. I didn't want to write a how-to column or give advice, but the idea of sharing my experiences honestly scared me to death. Yet in that inner realm where we sense our destiny, I felt I'd been chosen for a purpose.

Over the years, I've explored every aspect of my life, hoping to touch others by mirroring and reflecting upon our common experience. I've sought connection through the personal, inspired by Emerson: "In going down into the secrets of one's own mind, one descends into the secrets of all minds. The deeper one dives into one's most private presentiment, to one's wonder, one finds this is the most acceptable, most public and universally true. People delight in it; the better part of everyone feels, 'This is my music. This is myself.' "

The notes in my song are the particulars of my life — the family I have been given, the conversations I engage in, the tasks I undertake. The key may change from playful to sad, from silly to serious, but each column is a concert of sorts, filled with the tunes of others. I have a real husband named Jack, a mother-in-law, two daughters, parents, and siblings who find themselves on the pages of the newspaper, but never by surprise. With the exception of my father, I've made a point of sharing relevant passages with friends and family prior to publication, hoping that together we can understand what is taking place between us. As much as I strive to express the truth of my own experience, I wouldn't have been able to remain in relationship with those I love if I hadn't allowed them to appear as they see themselves.

Every once in a while I've picked up the phone and plunged into unfinished business. I called my brother to alert him to an angry column about my father, and he packed up his son and drove into Worcester to be with my dad when he opened the paper. When I shared a column about the lingering effects of childhood competition with my sister, we discovered that, without having realized it ourselves, we were both ready to move on. The struggles with my mother, which I shared so openly over the years, culminated in a breakthrough on the night my mother died.

Of course, none of us can ever be entirely truthful. Our view of the world is limited by our preconceptions. When we're faced with facts that don't fit, or tempted to overlook events that do not support our "story," we ignore the kind act in a world we consider cruel, or turn a husband's thoughtless remark into a barb. It's difficult, weaving a tale, to make sense of these loose ends.

Yet something fascinates me about jarring moments, those disturbing bits of reality that challenge our preconceived notions. My life would not seem to be fertile material for the hundreds of columns I've written over sixteen years — same house, same husband, same supermarket year after year — if it were not that I've tried to deal with life as it breaks through my defenses against it, disquieting, perplexing, and confounding me. I have offered up a life in process. I have shared, as faithfully as I can, the facts of my life and the sense I've tried to make of them. I believe, with contemporary poet Marc Weber, that "the vast ambiguity of life is its deepest truth."

Most people, I find, try to avoid the troubling aspects of relationships — the conflicts, the disappointments, and their own contribution to conflict and confusion. I've always headed straight for trouble like a swimmer heading into the breakers, convinced that I could handle the blow, whether it was to my ego, my vanity, or to my sense that, in order to be lovable, I had to be perfect. I trusted that smooth water lay just beyond the crashing waves. I had faith that my desire to love others more fully was the key to my own lovability. I came to this job with all the self-doubts and vulnerabilities of anyone on this earth, but I was determined to submit to the whole truth about myself. In the ebb and flow of these columns, I have been making peace with my flawed self and thereby finding the key to loving and accepting others.

Imperfection, after all, is the one thing all human beings share.

Sometimes it seems to me that we madly search the wide world for what is missing in our own lives, turning away from the people closest at hand to pursue, as Philip Slater, author of *Pursuit of Loneliness*, puts it: "the rich, vivid abundant life that is always elsewhere; always there, never here."

I have sought my happiness close to home.

I have not been disappointed.

Myself

July 1985

MY BEST FRIEND, LYNN, called me midway through the month. "We've got to get going. Time's running out," she said.

I knew exactly what she meant. Lynn was referring to the fact that we'd seriously fallen behind in meeting our Fun Quota.

Better known as F.Q.

Most people have a fun quota, whether they're aware of it or not. It's the source of that nagging sense that a perfectly sensible life is less than satisfying, the cause of a puzzling feeling of self-pity when everything seems to be going well. You can survive with the essentials — water, air, food, and shelter. You can glory in the extras — good health, love, and success. You can even fool yourself into thinking that money can bring happiness through expensive pleasures. But sooner or later, the five most forlorn words in the English language will pop into your head and refuse to go away: *I'm not having any fun.*

Having fun isn't quite the same as enjoying yourself or indulging yourself or being entertained, at least in my book. Having fun makes you feel that being alive is an absolute delight. Fun isn't *fun* unless it gets you back in touch with the kid inside who's never heard of limits or dignity or responsibility. In my opinion, fun is the one thing that makes being grown up bearable.

It's not easy to explain what's fun about fun, but it helps if you're breaking the rules in some way. Sometimes you only defy social conventions: *Obey "No Trespassing" signs. Always be polite. Don't talk to strangers.* But sometimes the rules come straight from your conscience: *You should be making better use of your time. If you can't do it right, don't do it at all. What will people think?*

Ah, how can I convey the feeling that comes when you stick your tongue out at that supercilious prig inside and become an outlaw? Suddenly a conversation with a total stranger makes you giggle. The lake, as you peel off your bathing suit, grows cooler and deeper. The trip you are taking on the spur of the moment hints that anything can happen. The concerns, which weigh down your other self who is always so good, lift like helium balloons. You're behaving like a kid again, acting on impulse, releasing pent-up energy. Out of character, out of line, you think to yourself, *I shouldn't be doing this at my age.* Then you know you're really having fun.

I'm convinced having fun serves a useful purpose in civilization, even if all it does is keep middle-aged ladies like me from running off and joining the circus.

Having fun, like sex, proceeds in stages. It begins with a devilish impulse, a feeling of freedom from constraint. Then comes a surge of playfulness, a rush of light-heartedness, and finally the climax — a smile, a grin, peals of laughter. You hope no one you know is watching. You suspect your peers would be shocked. The fact is that you can only have fun if the one who isn't judging you is you.

Of course, like sex, fun is better if you have someone to share it with, and so for the past twenty years Lynn and I have dedicated a significant portion of our time together to having fun. We specialize in cheap fun, dumb fun, immature fun. So we know exactly what to do when Lynn's internal F. Q. monitor sounds the alert that we are failing to meet our quota.

We rise at six in the morning and join a group waving political signs at sleepy commuters. We attend the opening ceremonies for a Buddhist Peace pagoda. October babies, we throw a birthday party for ourselves and ask our guests to come in costume as the old women they wish to become.

On this occasion, we decided to decorate our inner tubes.

Over the years Lynn and I have devised a way to carry on uninterrupted conversations while watching our children at the beach. We tie several inner tubes together, then paddle ourselves just far enough off shore so that in an emergency we can hear our kids call without being able to make out what they're saying. All afternoon we talk and drift, wasting hours of the day that could have been put to perfectly good use.

Since we live in a yachting community where staying afloat has been raised to a fine art, Lynn and I decided to name our inner tubes, and every summer we take a day to make them seaworthy, painting names and images on them with fluorescent paint.

One year, we christened our tubes the Boob, the Toothpaste,

and the Lipstick. The next year we named our tubes the Eustachian, the Bronchial, and the Fallopian, the last of which we decorated with a pair of glittering purple ovaries. The year our kids graduated from high school, we came up with the Amplitube, the Pulchritube, and, of course, the Scholastic Aptitube Test.

Unfortunately, we're getting a late start this year. So far, I have gold paint on my shopping list and only one name in my head — the Tuba. Lynn and I know it's silly to spend a morning this late in July decorating tubes that will deflate and go to the dump in September, but this task has one absolutely necessary redeeming characteristic.

It's fun.

February 1989

THE BASQUE HAVE A saying: To be successful at being human one should (1) show up; (2) pay attention; (3) tell the truth without judgment or blame; and (4) not be attached to the outcome.

When I first read that, I had to smile. Everything important is so simple as to be nearly impossible. Two years ago my friend Kaiya and I went to a telling-the-truth workshop, and I've been struggling with that third principle ever since.

I came to appreciate the truth later in life. When I was young, it was difficult to get my mother's attention, so I learned to take center stage by creating dramas. I became a skilled exaggerator. It took me years of therapy to see that my unembroidered self was worthy of attention. By the time I attended the workshop, though, I was proud of my hard-won honesty. I'd learned to see the drama in my life without having to distort the truth. I answered questions with thoughtful, honest answers. I'd rid myself of the impulse to tell lies, but fibs — tricky little social omissions and evasions — were still part of my life.

At the end of the workshop, Kaiya and I agreed we'd meet weekly for breakfast and work on the falsehoods we told without even noticing, the excuses we made up because they sounded better than our real reasons. I pointed out when she smoothed things over with plausible explanations. She called attention to my use of little white lies. After a while, I began to catch myself.

For example, I wanted to attend a Town Meeting scheduled on the same night as an important meeting at church. I called to talk my way out of it.

"Bill, I'm not feeling well," I fibbed, but when I hung up, the pretense bothered me. I called back. "Listen," I said, "I'm not coming because I want to go to Town Meeting." When I mentioned the issues in question, Bill decided to switch the date of the meeting so we could all go.

Positive reinforcement like that gave me the courage to try again. This time a friend invited my husband and me to a series of discussions held at a local restaurant. The first night, the bill came to almost fifty dollars, more than Jack and I would choose to spend on a casual Sunday evening. We decided not to continue. I was assigned the task of calling to explain.

Bringing up the topic of money sounded awful to my ears, like pleading poverty. What excuse wouldn't make me sound like a cheapskate? None that was truthful. I dialed the number and blurted out: "Sorry. It's too expensive." After a moment of silence, our friend was very pleasant. He must not have felt too critical because he and his wife invited me over for lunch a week later.

The more I practice, the better I get — which helps, because situations keep getting stickier. This fall, for example, my friend Lynn and I were planning to drive together to the Globe Book Festival where I was scheduled to give a talk, when two other friends asked to come along. I like them a lot, and I was happy to drive them. The problem was that Lynn and I were meeting someone for lunch first, and I didn't want to bring two extra people along.

"What can we say?" I asked Lynn, who'd been following my truth-telling saga closely. We racked our brains for a story that wouldn't hurt their feelings, but everything sounded farfetched. We even considered inviting them to lunch, but then Lynn and I looked at each other and knew it was time for the truth again.

"Listen," I said to our two friends, "Lynn and I are meeting someone for lunch. Do you mind if we go off for an hour?"

"No problem. We'll window shop." And that was the end of it.

Telling the truth is fun when you get the hang of it. By-and-large people respond to the truth without much fuss. They're not half as vulnerable as my imagination makes them. Best of all, those lies that would otherwise live on in me as body tension give way to a relaxed, unguarded ease that makes me easier to get along with.

I've come to see that my truth isn't usually hurtful, either. I care about the people in my life; that's why they're there. It follows that my honest feelings are rarely a condemnation of them. Since I do things for the same reasons other people do, why did I ever believe that no one would understand? I've come to see that this web of social lies clutters the space between friends — and in families — creating a distance no one truly wants.

Take this call from my daughter Julie: "You know what was the nicest thing about last night's dinner? That I could tell you I didn't like the rice."

"Was that hard to do?" I asked.

"I didn't want to hurt your feelings, especially if you'd gone to a lot of bother, but I thought, 'She knows I think she's a good cook, so why shouldn't I say what I think?' You know what I mean?"

"Absolutely," I said.

Perhaps the best thing about the truth is that it's contagious.

July 1989

AM I A FEMINIST? Of course, I am. I'm surprised how many of my readers think that anyone who doesn't have a full-time career outside the home can't possibly be a feminist.

"I like that you celebrate the old-fashioned values we held before women's lib," one of them wrote me recently. I didn't know how to respond. Is wanting to nurture old-fashioned because that feeling's been around so long? Or is caring for others as up-to-date as you can get?

I do celebrate some traditionally female values. I also put a lot of energy into my relationships, and if those aren't going well, my professional achievements offer little consolation. In these ways, my life may resemble a time "before women's lib," but there's really no comparison . . . because I have a choice.

Isn't that what the liberation of women is all about?

My mother, for example, gave up paid work after she married. She briefly transcribed books into Braille, studied oil painting, and volunteered, none of which seemed to mean very much to her. Still, she was supposed to be satisfied with being a housewife, and if she wasn't, it was understood there was something wrong with her.

I was at home with a new infant when I first read Betty Friedan's book *The Feminine Mystique*. What that book said to me was that there was more to life than domesticity, that the larger world ought to be open to any woman who wished to enter it. As I understood it, the aim of women's liberation was to open those doors, not to push every female on earth through them, whether she wanted to go or not.

In theory, as barriers to women in the workplace fell, those women who wanted to work were to be free to enter what had previously been considered a man's domain, and women in traditionally female jobs were to be paid wages that reflected the importance of their work. Those women who didn't need to work were to be free, too — to do as they pleased. As for men, there was the clear expectation that, as they began to recognize what rigid categories they'd been forced to work within, they'd find their niche at home.

It all seems incredibly naïve now.

What actually happened was that women slipped easily into new work roles. Paid work, after all, offered financial rewards, a clear path of advancement, and adult companionship, all of which domestic life lacked. For men, however, there was no prestige attached to changing diapers. Too much time at home was more apt to threaten a man's chances for advancement and lower his status. As for rewards, an overworked wife was bound to take her mate's contribution for granted, and the baby more likely to spit up on Dad than pat him on the back.

Is it any wonder, then, that the effects have been so one-sided? There was every incentive for women to walk away from home and none for men to step into that void — leaving women to assume a double burden, at work and at home, in order to sustain family life.

In a culture that has consistently discredited and devalued women's activities, it's important that someone stand up and proclaim the importance and pleasure of nurturing. How can there be true equality of the sexes unless the skills once solely associated with the female gender are deemed worthy of respect? Until we recover the sacred dimension of women's traditional life, home will be no more than the place men and women have to go when the important work of the day is over.

And the world will be the poorer for it.

Someone needs to celebrate the art of home-making, to demonstrate the necessity, as well as the rewards, of exercising our capacity to nourish and love one another. Distinct from the sex that practices it, this society needs a "*human* mystique," one that understands that shelter and comfort and warmth, as well as safety and security, are of profound importance to the development of happy, productive human beings. The hand that rocks the cradle contributes to the world's destiny as surely as the hand that presses the computer key.

My defense of the choice to be at home validates the right of every person to pursue his or her own fulfillment. I've been a research assistant, an elementary school teacher, and an assistant editor, but at the moment I am choosing to stay attuned to the rhythms of my household and to struggle with all the issues domesticity brings up for me.

Besides making me a feminist, it makes all the difference.

MY HUSBAND, JACK, my daughter Julie, and I went up to our land in Vermont last weekend to work on the shelter we've been building for the past few summers. My sciatic nerve was bothering me, so I didn't intend to offer more than moral support, but it was dark, and so I helped lug the sleeping bags into the house. In the morning we began putting in a pine floor, which meant that while two of us hammered, a third was needed to push the boards close together. I couldn't decide which task would put less stress on my back, so I alternated, hammering while on my hands and knees, then bracing a board with my shoe.

It took three of us to lift a foam mattress into the loft so, of course, I did my part, and after Jack and Julie cooked the meals over the campfire, it seemed only fair for me to squat by our stream and wash the dishes. I rested in the back seat of the car on the way home, but after we unpacked our borrowed Jeep, it was too dirty to return without a cleaning. Jack looked so tired I couldn't let him wash it alone. While he scrubbed the exterior, I kept him company by doing the inside.

By the time I got to bed Sunday night, I felt as if I'd spent a week on the rack. Now that the pain in my leg finally had my attention, it was screaming at me: *What do you think you're doing? Are you crazy?*

I couldn't think of a thing to say in my own defense.

I hadn't meant to hurt myself, but somehow I'd lost touch with my ability to protect myself. Some other imperative had taken precedence over self-interest. It wasn't external pressure, either. In fact, Jack and Julie had frequently asked, "Are you sure you feel well enough to do this?" and I'd insisted that I did. Clearly, something more powerful than a commitment to my well-being was controlling my behavior.

Claudia Bepko and Jo-Ann Krestan in their book *Too Good for Her Own Good* would say that I was following the hypnotic Code of Goodness, which they believe shapes a woman's sense of who she is. In order to feel good about themselves, they maintain, many women find it necessary to act against their own best interests. One of the rules in their code fit my case exactly: Be unselfish and of service.

How do they know that my sense of whether I am worthy of love requires that I carry my own weight? I feel compelled to pitch in when there's work to do. I'm convinced the worst thing anyone could say about me is that I'm lazy or self-indulgent. I can't seem to feel good about myself unless I respond when other people need me. If I don't feel good about myself, I feel as if I can't expect or allow anyone else to feel good about me, either.

I should be awarded the Code of Goodness Seal of Honor.

This doesn't always get me into trouble. I enjoy helping most of the time, and I usually feel appreciated, but when meeting everyone else's needs takes precedence over my own, I often feel as if my only escape would be to run away. I won't let myself quit, yet I resent that I'm the only one in this family who's not allowed to stop when I'm tired. I'm often angry that I have to work so hard. Where do these imperatives come from? Why can't I see that "not allowed" and "have to" are my own creations? That what I have to escape from is the tyranny of my own standards?

"If you feel bad any time you fail to achieve these qualities perfectly, it may be a signal that you're trapped by the Code of Goodness," write Bepko and Krestan. "You may be too good for your own good."

I'm listening. With a summer of Vermont weekends ahead, I'll have many chances to shift my emphasis from *doing* good to *feeling* good. It's time to acknowledge how much everyone else contributes without feeling guilty that I'm not doing more than my share. It's time to be more approving of others than angry at myself, time to replace my pride in my own competence with a full measure of gratitude for everyone else's contribution.

I think I've caught a glimpse of another pathway to love in this, one that may serve me better than any Code of Goodness. Perhaps I can now concentrate on giving love to others instead of always trying to earn it for myself.

September 1991
I HAD ONE OF THE WORST colds of my life. I blew my way through a box of Kleenex, flopping about in bed like a Raggedy Ann doll, convinced that if I lay flat, I'd drown in my own body fluids. As day became night, I roused myself only long enough to take an occasional sip of water. I rose after a sleepless night, too exhausted to rally. As I tried to brush my teeth without asphyxiating myself, my mind had its first clear thought in twenty-four hours.

I haven't eaten anything.

My chapped lips parted in an involuntary smile. Nice to think I might lose a few pounds. This was the silver lining to my infectious cloud. *Something good has to come out of everything,* I told myself. I fell back into bed and didn't have another thought until my husband invited me downstairs for dinner. He'd made bluefish, baked potato, and corn, and this nutritious food sat on my plate, looking delicious, though God knows, not to me. I stared at it for a while, watching my husband eat. We didn't talk. There was a bully chattering away in my head, and she required my full attention.

"I don't have to eat," she mocked. "I'm in charge of this body, not a slave to it like you."

I knew whom she was addressing — the part of me without will power, the hungry little pig who can't resist a piece of cake if it's set before her, the one who screws up every diet she's ever tried.

"I don't have to touch this," the voice taunted. "I'm not weak. I'm not needy. I can't be tempted." There was contempt in her words and barely contained disgust. She reached for the glass of water and took a long drink. "I'm full," she announced. "I'm done."

I excused myself and went upstairs, surprised at how elated I was. I felt complete and powerful in spite of my cold. How easy it is to set yourself against food. Just one powerful NO, instead of a thousand daily decisions, a million daily capitulations. Toast or bagel? Neither. Fish or chicken? Nothing, thank you. No more filling up that embarrassing void three times a day, no more guilt after eating normally.

I had thickened around the middle, hadn't I? My stomach stuck out, didn't it? My appetite had destroyed the slimness I valued so highly. My eating felt out of my control, even if I only "pigged out" on healthy food. Until I went almost two days without eating, I'd never realized how compromised I felt after every single meal.

"We'll have nothing but coffee for breakfast — unless you cave in," my storm trooper whispered. "Give me a week or two. You'll be thin again."

I wanted to become slim and graceful. I hate that every calorie I eat shows up on my body for everyone to see. By now I was painfully in touch with the shame I seem to attach to my desire to eat. How had I ever come to consider this awful feeling so ordinary and so unremarkable?

I used to think people with eating disorders were different from me. Anorexia was for adolescents in a power struggle with their parents. Bulimia affected people obsessed with their looks. What person in her right mind would starve herself past gauntness? What kind of woman would stick her fingers down her throat so often the enamel on her teeth rotted? What sort of idiot would think her middle-aged body, no matter how starved, could ever resemble a fashion model's?

More than two thousand years ago, the Roman philosopher Terence said, "Nothing human is alien to me." I wonder what it was that he caught a glimpse of inside himself. I may be middle-aged, married, and not at risk for an eating disorder, but, like Terence, I know that this illness, which has been called the female disorder of our age, lurks in me, too.

I'm not giving in to it. This morning I ate. Then I judged myself. Then I forgave myself. What else can any of us do?

November 1991

THIS CULTURE IS FULL of repulsive words used to describe the elderly: fuddy duddy, fossil, biddy, dingbat, hag. For effect, you can string them together in horrid phrases, like "doddering old codger" and "wizened old witch." I was contemplating this list of epithets at a workshop called "Ourselves, Growing Older," given at Framingham Union

Hospital, when I came across one of my favorite words: "Crone."

Doesn't it sound strong? Doesn't it remind you of that mysterious old lady in fairy tales who intervenes and always saves the day? Some sources think the word comes from *carogne*, a medieval French word meaning "cantankerous or mischievous woman." Others think it's derived from the Greek *chronios*, meaning "long-lasting." Crone has great roots.

Seeing that word again brought back memories of the year my best friend, Lynn, and I, both born in October, decided to invite our friends to a joint birthday party.

The invitations read: "Let your crone hang out!"

I had just read an essay by Ursula LeGuin on why the best person to welcome extraterrestrials, should they land and ask for our "leader," would be a wise old granny. Back in those days, P. L. Travers, the author of *Mary Poppins*, was writing, "Don't shunt me off to Florida, angels, or make me a senior citizen. Give me, when the time comes, the crown of being a crone." And Mary Daly, in her trail-blazing book *Gyn/Ecology*, had defined crones as the "long-lasting ones," whose survival gave testimony to their courage, strength, and judgment. Everywhere I looked, it seemed, feminists were attempting to reclaim the word "crone" as a way of championing the wisdom of old women.

Lynn and I chose to go to our party as polar opposites. Lynn epitomized the dark vision that haunts women in this culture. She blacked out two front teeth, and layered several outfits she had scooped up from her closet floor. With a ripped straw hat and a shopping bag filled with the contents of one of her drawers, she became the discarded, sorry old woman we call a "bag lady."

Inspired by the defiance of women like Mary Daly, I wanted to express my resistance to the idea of outliving my usefulness. I wrapped my head in a colorful scarf, put on too much jewelry, wore a ruffled shirt with a skirt made from an Indian bedspread, put on the brightest lipstick I could find, and overdid the eye shadow. I was aiming for the female counterpart to Zorba the Greek.

The morning of the party I woke up with a poem full-blown in my head, and I read it after Lynn and I blew out our firestorm of birthday candles.

What Is a Crone?

A little old lady who refuses to shrink,
Who continues to say whatever she thinks,
Who hasn't a feeling she tries to disown —
That's what it means to grow into a crone.

A woman whose body is just excess baggage,
Who doesn't concern herself with the saggage,
Whose pride in her figure is not overblown —
That's who it is who grows into a crone.

See all the wisdom she's gained with the years,
All the compassion that came with the tears,
Yearning for impact right down to the bone —
That's what it means to turn into a crone.

Look at the children who sprang from her womb,
Look how she thumbs her long nose at the tomb,
Laughter and wisecracks, wit, not a moan —
There's a spark in the lady who longs to be crone.

Many the subjects she's longing to learn,
So much of love she still needs to return,
She's one of a kind; she is never a clone —
She's a woman in training on how to be crone.

Look at her reading with magnifying glass,
Look at her spewing out volumes of sass,
Time may have passed, but this lady's not prone —
There's power and promise in being a crone.

Give her a flower to stick in her hair,
Something outrageous that she'd like to wear,
Say she's flamboyant, her taste has all flown —
She'll say she's become the quintessence of crone.

I seem to become more outrageous with every birthday, as if the force of convention that keeps us all acting alike loses more of its power over me with every passing year. I have a clear picture of what I'm aiming to become as my body slowly wrinkles me into a crone: more and more myself.

October 1993

I BEGAN WRITING at a table just off the kitchen. Though my daughters were both in school, interruptions flourished like mold in my refrigerator. I ended up reading the paper, answering the phone, doing the dishes, and watering plants, anything to avoid putting words on paper.

Then I'd berate myself for not accomplishing anything.

A short reminiscence of mine in the *Boston Globe Magazine* gave me my first big chance. A book editor saw it and asked me to turn it into a novel for young adults. Finding it difficult to work at home, I moved my office to an empty room in a local church and made myself go there three times a week. Eventually, I developed a method for getting myself to buckle down. I'd start by editing the rough draft of the day before, then, re-immersed in the story, produce a few more pages of copy. It took me a year to write the one-hundred-forty-five pages of *Beginning to Feel the Magic*.

I wrote my next book, the novelization of a TV series called "The New Voice," in a real office at WGBH-TV. I was beginning to trust my ability to motivate myself, so when that book was done, I moved home. I'd read Virginia Woolf's *A Room of My Own* in college and now, years later, I actually had my own space in an extra bedroom, even if I shared it with a sewing machine, piles of fabric, an ironing board, and wrinkled clothes. I made a desk from a door, bought a computer, and settled in. Despite the chaos, with the door shut I could work undisturbed for hours.

The room had only one window. Well, I wasn't there to look at scenery. When cold drafts whipped across the floor all winter, I plugged in a heater and dressed more warmly. I was thrilled to have what writers have — a place set aside for work. I was overjoyed to do what writers do — I worked at my craft almost every day. Therefore, I told myself, I was a writer.

A writer, of course, who ran errands, cooked dinner, and cleaned house in addition to my professional tasks. Like most working women, I always had too much to do, but I thought this was the way it was supposed to be, that you just kept throwing one ball after another into the air even though you never grew another hand. You juggled, you struggled, you thanked your lucky stars for meaningful work, no matter how tired you were at the end of the day. I didn't feel I deserved help. After all, I already had a cleaning lady. I never considered renovating my office. How could I complain when I had four solid walls and a door that shut? How could I justify indulging myself when I was already luckier than I deserved?

Then I ran into a friend who ran a business from home — only this friend was a man. Stunned, I listened to him talk of his support staff. He had a secretary, a bookkeeper, an accountant, three consultants, and a wife. He showed me his home office. It looked like a place where work was taken seriously. Why did I treat my writing as a private passion, to be fit into my life as unobtrusively as possible? Why did it take me twelve years of steady employment to see that I was actually running a small business myself?

The first thing I did after this revelation was to hire an assistant to come in one afternoon a week to help me answer mail, make copies of my columns, and run errands. All week long I'd set things aside for her to do. When I looked at her clipboard, I'd thank my lucky stars that I had someone I could depend upon to help me out. Then I paid attention to other things, like my office. I didn't like its color. I didn't like being cold all winter, either, or having books tumbling off the crowded shelves, or having my workspace cluttered with mending and ironing. I had too little storage space, too few work surfaces, not enough light. In my new frame of mind, I asked myself a question: What would a man do?

Then I did it.

The workmen have left and I sit here, getting used to my new surroundings. The carpenters took down a wall and doubled my space. They built cabinets, with extensive counter space, under large new windows that overlook our yard. They put in floor-to-ceiling bookcases. I now have a chair for visitors to sit on, a hibiscus plant in bloom, and creamy peach walls. I even had a friend paint clouds on the ceiling so that two seagulls now soar in the sky above my head.

This is the first time I've written in a room that is my own in every way. I was grateful for my first office. I'm overjoyed with this one. I'm beginning to feel I belong here.

In fact, I'm going to change that first sentence, "I began writing at a table . . ." Sitting here with all the tools of my trade in full view, I think it should read, "My career as a writer began . . ."

January 1996

I GAVE A TALK at Harvard Divinity School this fall. When I finished speaking, the audience gave me a standing ovation. As I stood looking out at the crowd, I felt I had finally reached a new stage in my life.

I was proud of myself, but not for the reason you'd think. Of course, I was thrilled the audience liked my talk, but what was even more amazing was that I was able to take in their approval and feel good about it. The topic of my speech had been breaking out of destructive childhood patterns. Taking delight in their positive reaction may have been my biggest break of all with the past.

When I was a young girl, my parents taught me, without actually putting it into words, that the good things you get are taken from somebody else.

It worked like this: It seemed that the person who was first in the class made everyone else second-rate. The girls in cashmere sweaters caused the rest of us to feel poor, while the popular girls made everyone else's lack of a social life unbearable. This kind of "theft" was a universal law, like the pull of gravity. And it got worse over time.

All through high school I lived in fear that someone else would get my place at a top college, win the glamorous well-paying job I wanted, and marry the man who'd be perfect for me. Everywhere, it seemed, people were racing ahead of me toward my goals. In my fierce desire to compete and win, I was, of course, trying to beat them to it.

My operative emotion was envy. As a teen-ager, I kept a sharp eye on who was winning the prizes I wanted: Honor Roll. Class officer. Yearbook editor. Lead in the senior play. Prettiest. Best figure. Most self-assured. Miss Popularity. On and on and on I went, comparing myself unfavorably to some perfect teen who was a figment of my imagination. The most damaging aspect of the process, however, was my conviction that there wasn't enough good to go around, as if, after the lucky few got their pick, there'd be nothing left — no good men, no good colleges, no good jobs, no worthwhile ways to spend a life.

I was resentful because I imagined every one of those girls thought they were better than I was. My adolescence was one part envy, one part anger, and one part self-hatred. I was in a no-win situation without knowing it because if by some fluke I ever succeeded, I was bound to be blamed and resented by people just like me. After all, I wasn't glad for anyone who excelled. I certainly didn't learn from them or care about them, so what could I expect? If I ever gained anything worth envying, I was sure I'd be surrounded by people who felt diminished by my success and whose secret wish would be to see me fail. And I'd feel bad about having stolen their thunder.

It was a chilling scenario. I grew up believing it was simply the way the world worked.

It took me a long time to learn that there isn't just one prize worth having in this world. One person's idea of an exciting challenge is another person's burnout; your piece of cake can be my worst nightmare. Ask around. Whatever flaws there are in our lives, few of us would be willing to trade our problems for someone else's.

In fact, the older I've gotten, the more impossible the whole idea of trading places seems. I no longer feel like a needy child waiting for Santa Claus to hand me something from his limited supply of goodies. I've come to believe that, as a flower emerges from a seed, every life unfolds by some inner necessity and takes its shape from its innermost being. As I see it now, life isn't so much a competition as a God-given opportunity for each of us to become our own best self.

From that perspective, I now see my audience as well-wishers who have no reason to begrudge me success on my journey. In turn, my sense that my life is uniquely and appropriately mine allows me to feel good when the people around me succeed. It's the sense that we're each traveling our own unique path into the future that makes it possible to support and cheer another on her way, because in trying to become your best self, you never steal anyone else's glory.

How could you? As long as people come equipped with hands, there'll be more than enough applause to go around.

February 1997

IT WAS LATE AFTERNOON and I felt restless. I wanted to talk to someone, but to whom? I reached for the phone, then stopped, stood up and looked out my office window at two crows strutting in my darkening yard. I felt disconnected and in distress for no reason. Then I recognized the emotion I was feeling. In fact I even knew its name. Strangely enough, I identified my feeling as loneliness with a sigh of relief. I think it signaled the end of a prolonged period of grieving.

Two years ago, when my closeness to my best friend, Lynn, came to an end, I was in a state of shock. It seemed hard to believe that years of intimacy could simply vanish into thin air, but after an argument in Lynn's kitchen and an exchange of letters in which we held nothing back, Lynn and I agreed that our friendship was essentially over. We parted more in sadness than in anger. We still see each other occasionally, but wind whistles through the space between us.

This is my best understanding of what happened: During the years Lynn's husband has been suffering from Parkinson's Disease, I viewed myself as a resource for Lynn when she needed time away from caretaking. I listened and offered sympathy, but I also tried to distract her, to be a counterbalance to the concerns that weighed her down.

From my point of view, I saw myself as helpful and supportive. From Lynn's perspective, however, my phone calls and visits had begun to feel like additional demands on her time and energy. She experienced me as wanting something from her at a time when she didn't feel there was enough of her to go around. Being a mother, a wife, and a caretaker felt like all she could handle without having to deal with pressure from me to be a best friend as well.

Besides, I didn't understand her situation. My husband wasn't sick. I hadn't given up my job. I didn't have to make choices that seemed obvious only to someone whose lifeboat was in danger of capsizing. Our paths had diverged, and what did I know about sleepless nights and medical disappointments and the pull of promises made years ago? Lynn despaired of my ever being able to comprehend the ways in which everything had shifted due to the changes in her life.

Suddenly it became clear how unbalanced our relationship had become. For a long while, my concerns had seemed so insignificant compared to hers that I rarely mentioned them. For a long while, she'd been annoyed that I was questioning her solutions to problems I hadn't experienced myself. We stared at each other over a gulf that seemed to have appeared out of nowhere, but in fact our love for one another had kept us from acknowledging that we'd been slowly moving further and further away from meeting one another's needs for a long time.

I never thought anything could come between the two of us. We'd fit together like a hand and glove through so many crises that we'd lost track of the fact that we were actually two individuals who could be altered by time and history. We thought we were in charge of our personal destinies and never realized the power that fate and fortune held over our lives. Like two carefree swimmers who are unaware that the water in which they swim hides currents with the power to carry them to very different destinations, we didn't understand that our needs and desires could shift in response to circumstances. We didn't know that forces other than our own conscious choices could affect our ability to remain in relationship.

I wish we were back in Victorian times when heterosexual women were unashamed of the powerful bond between friends because then it would seem less strange for me to admit to a thirty-year love affair with a person of my own sex. I will never forget the depth of communion between us or the way our deepest selves entwined, enriching both our lives. I have been immeasurably strengthened by our years together. I look back not with regret, but with gratitude.

It's the present that has me in mourning.

"You are called to live out of a new place," says Henri Nouwen in his journal of a broken heart called *The Inner Voice of Love: A Journey Through Anguish to Freedom.* "You are being asked to trust . . . that your experience of emptiness is not the final experience . . . "

The yard is desolate. The crows have fled with the last light, but though I can see no visible signs of warmer weather, I know that nature's bleakness is both temporary and illusory. Seeds are waiting in the frozen ground. New sap will soon be flowing through the trees. This is my time to patiently inhabit the wintry places in my soul until spring comes.

June 1997

SOMETIMES YOU GET to a point in your life when you hit the wall of "one too many." One more phone call, one more commitment, one more problem, and you'll break. One more bill, one more decision, one more change, and you'll fall apart. Your skin feels stretched to the limit over your bones. Your brain presses painfully against your skull. Your memory refuses to absorb one more bit of information. You feel tired of life, yet you go to bed tense and wake up anxious, your list still buzzing in your mind like an angry swarm of bees. Beset by too much to do, you can't seem to focus on any one thing long enough to actually enjoy doing it. At the end of a productive day, you can't recall a single accomplishment worth remembering, and you can't help thinking that Alexander Solzhenitsyn was right in saying that all our progress has turned out to be "an insane, ill-considered, furious dash into a blind alley."

When I find myself *en route* to this particular dead end, all I feel is the numbness of disconnection.

That's when I head off to the Option Institute, a personal growth center in Western Massachusetts, for a week of provocation and reflection. I need to break out of the habits of mind that are driving me down this road. I need time to think and to be coached one more time in how to create a meaningful world from the inside.

On my first morning there, those of us in the workshop were presented with a rack of costumes. I put on a superman costume with a flowing red cape. It suited me to look so streamlined and unassailable while I felt so flat and empty inside. I managed to remain detached and undisturbed as other people shared their painful dilemmas.

After a few hours, we were asked to change costumes. I came back as a convict, wearing black-and-white striped pajamas. This time I felt the constriction of overload, as if I'd been tied to a grindstone for weeks. Suddenly, I was aware that personal phone calls were at the bottom of my list, "allowed" only after everything else was completed. I was no longer making time for walks with a partner, or had energy for a cup of coffee after a meeting, or felt up to inviting folks for dinner. All my nurturing relationships had been relegated to the category of "one too many" in my already too busy life.

"How do you want to be in the world?" asked Barry Neil Kaufman, the Director of the Option Institute, and suddenly the floodgates broke. I'd been a model of efficiency, lost in a whirl of scattered thoughts. Now, five hours into our first session, I began crying. I felt human again. I welcomed the intensity of my pain and sadness. I could breathe deeply. I could long for companionship again.

I came home, determined to change my pattern. Within a week, one of my favorite women dropped by to give me a copy of her newly published book of poems. "Stay for coffee," I said, delighted to find I'd left space in my schedule for an unexpected encounter, but she had too many other stops to make and rushed away.

A week later, another wonderful woman came by to give me a copy of a poem of mine she'd calligraphied as a gift. "Can you stay for a cup of coffee?" I asked, excited by the opportunity to get to know her better, but she had errands to run before a dentist appointment and dashed off.

I'll probably never have a heart-to-heart talk with either of them.

Because we're all too busy. Overstressed and overextended, we deny that there are limits to how hard we can push ourselves before we're undone by our own unmet needs for other people. In our rush to succeed, to consume, and to accomplish, we are busily burning the bridges that connect us to supportive family relationships, a network of friends, and the feeling of belonging to a caring community.

"We must have some room to breathe. We need freedom to think and permission to heal. Our relationships are being starved to death by velocity. No one has the time to listen, let alone love," says Richard A. Swenson, in his disturbing book *Margin: Restoring Emotional, Physical, Financial, and Time Reserve to Overloaded Lives.*

What is the point in our being here? Are we so focused on work, on efficiency, on making and spending money that we're willing to sacrifice the social, emotional, and spiritual dimensions of our lives? How do we want to be in the world? How long can we keep running away from that question?

"Must we love?" Swenson asks. "That is a nonsensical question. It is like asking, 'Must we breathe?' No, we do not have to breathe and no, we do not have to love. But the consequences of both those decisions will be the same."

September 1997

I'M SPENDING THESE DAYS in limbo, recovering from a painful case of shingles.

Limbo, it turns out, is a place without details. It's the absence of ordinary activity — no errands or phone calls, no cooking, cleaning, meetings, shopping, or dentist's appointments. It's the cancellation of events I've been anticipating — a weekend in Vermont, a workshop I was looking forward to attending, a presentation I'd prepared for the women of a national association visiting Boston.

Limbo is a siphon into my body, where all that matters is the next codeine, what's for lunch, and whether the video my husband's chosen can hold my attention for ten whole minutes. It's utter passivity, the loss of interest in everything and anything outside my skin. My mind curls up into a fetal position somewhere as far from pain as my imagination can take it, to a place without words or thoughts where the life force barely simmers.

Carlos Casteneda says death is with us always, perching on our shoulder, but limbo feels more like death's waiting room, like confinement in a no-man's land just a few feet from death's door. These past three weeks, I would not have been that surprised to see it open.

They say that no one on their death-bed ever regretted not spending more time at the office, and yet, I wonder, what do people regret at times like these? When they think back to when life was normal, what is it they wish they had a chance to do over? That question seems vitally important because one of the gifts a temporary illness brings is the opportunity to re-enter one's life with a new perspective.

I will have a chance to start afresh.

I swear there'll be no more petty self-recriminations. In the continual conversation we all carry on with ourselves, I regret every minute I have given over to reproving myself for trivial matters, like my five extra pounds, my forgetfulness, or my messiness. I could dwell on my faults forever, or for that matter, on the shortcomings of others, but what purpose has either one ever served but to dampen my spirits?

Annie Dillard says in her book *The Writing Life*, "How we spend our days is, of course, how we spend our lives." I need to learn that each day will be an acceptable jumble of good and bad, and shift my focus to something more fulfilling. As I lie on the couch, waiting for the pain in my arm to subside, waves of regret sweep through me, but not for any acts I have done or omitted in my lifetime.

What I regret most deeply is my own inability to sustain happiness for any length of time.

I have written of the euphoria that comes when we recognize, not only intellectually but in the deepest recesses of our hearts, the abundance of love in the universe. I have shared moments when my heart has soared. I have been given so much, yet it seems as if

I have willfully abandoned that ecstasy of recognition time and again in order to return to a world ruled by my own attachment to self-doubt and grievances. Like a bird rushing back into her cage, I voluntarily pick up my sack of woes as if happiness itself were too great a burden for me to carry. I have been a coward. I have been afraid to give myself permission to rejoice.

The reasons for this decision are somewhere in my childhood, but old habits can be broken. I can learn to bear the uneasiness I feel when I acknowledge that I am loved. I can endure the discomfort of basking in my own approval. I can stop interfering with my feelings of well-being.

When my life is given back to me, I do not want to squander the remaining portion of it.

Joseph Campbell has said, "We talk about seeking a meaning for life . . . I think that what we're really seeking is an experience of being alive, so that our life experiences on the physical plane resonate within our innermost being, so that we actually feel the rapture of being alive."

Rapture is the possibility our existence on earth holds out to us, a possibility so intense that it attracts and frightens us at the same time. This is the original blessing that attends every birth, and if there is sin, surely it consists of throwing away the effervescence that is our birthright.

My Mother's Daughter

THE PRESSURE FOR upward mobility is unrelenting in this culture, but no one talks about the psychic price paid by those who rise above their class.

I remember when my cousin Jerry, the first grandchild in our extended family to go to college, made plans one weekend to come home with a friend. He called beforehand to ask his mom a favor: "Could you put top sheets on the beds?"

That was the first I'd ever heard of having a sheet between sleeper and blanket. I remember overhearing my mother and my aunts talking about this insult which, I gathered, was a slap in the face to all of us. Whatever pride the family had taken in Jerry's accomplishments turned to ashes with this change in his character. *Who did he think he was?* He was ashamed of us all, obviously. It was clear that going to college had convinced him he was better than we were.

Sixteen, and soon to follow in Jerry's footsteps, I listened carefully. When I set off for college a year later, I was determined not to hurt my parents like he had. I'd have given anything for a polite, restrained dad like the ones the other girls produced at Sophomore Father's Day, but I gritted my teeth and hid my misgivings. After I got engaged, I reassured my mom that my fiancé's parents would be perfectly comfortable coming to our tiny house for dinner, though those words tasted like soap in my mouth.

After I married, I wanted my parents to feel that my house was always open to them, and, knowing that my mother took great pride in my every success, I took her into my confidence. I told her everything she wanted to know, including the price we'd paid for every piece of furniture. One day I came home to find my mother giving a house tour to a friend, describing all my bargains to the penny.

I bit my tongue until it swelled up and almost choked me. I wished she'd called before coming over, but I couldn't tell her that, could I? I wished she'd let me treat her and her friends like guests, but how could I impose a more formal structure on our relationship without hurting her? As a kid, I'd gotten A's for her, won swimming medals for her, published poems for her — and it hadn't killed me.

Why couldn't I leave things the way they'd always been? Did my annoyance mean I was starting to feel superior to my family? Wasn't the fact that she might think so reason enough to keep silent?

No one warns women about how conflicted we can feel about having a nicer house, a thinner body, or a more loving husband than our mothers had. No one tells us how guilty we can feel about a career that gives us the recognition our mothers never received. In therapy I discovered that, as I child, I'd made a vow not to be happy until my mother was, and this was how I kept my promise: I allowed myself to succeed beyond my mother's wildest dreams as long as I didn't allow myself to enjoy it. I hadn't let my good fortune make me happy, but as a grown woman with a life of my own, a mother myself, I had to break out of that pattern.

My mother was nervous when I dragged her upstairs on her next visit, saying I had to talk with her about something important. I stumbled. I hesitated. Finally, I managed to blurt out that I wanted her to call before she came over.

"Is that all?" she said, with a sigh of relief. "I was afraid you were going to ask me never to come back." That took my breath away. What had I ever done to make my mother actually think, or fear, that I might banish her forever?

I'm lucky my mother and I have been given enough time to make a continuous series of corrections in the course we are so awkwardly charting together. I'm grateful that my mother's love for her children is stronger than the discomfort into which our differences sometimes plunge us. I can write about our struggle to grow closer with such honesty because of her incredible generosity of spirit and because she's the quintessential Jewish mother,

She never minds a word I write about her.

As long as it gets published.

May 1985

WE WERE ALL HAVING breakfast at the Driftwood restaurant, my husband and I, our friends Mary Kay and David, and Mary Kay's parents who were visiting from Minnesota. When it came time to pay the bill, Mary Kay's dad automatically reached for the check.

"Wait a minute," Mary Kay said, gently restraining him. "We're all peers here. We'll pay our own way."

"We're too big to be taken care of by our mommies and daddies," I said, "and we've been too big since we turned forty."

We all laughed, but I was only half-joking. It takes a long time to stop being dependent, especially when the folks we depend on refuse to discourage us.

My friend Bonnie, who's in her mid-thirties, describes it this way: "When I leave my parents after a visit, my mom always takes me aside and presses twenty dollars into my hand, saying, 'This will help you get home.' "

Another friend explains, "My folks want me to visit them, and I can't afford it, so we've got this deal that works out to everyone's satisfaction: They pay and I come."

After all, kids get used to allowances and special treats, and parents like the feeling of magnanimity that comes from giving an unrequested (though not necessarily unexpected) gift. In some ways, it makes everyone feel good to hold on ever-so-marginally to familiar roles, even if it has to be done surreptitiously.

"I always make money going out to dinner with my folks," says Sandra, a woman from our church. "Not only do they pick up the check, but without telling each other, everyone, including my grandparents, slips me a ten dollar bill under the table."

"I find money in my wallet when I get home," my neighbor Carol confesses.

"I refused to take money from my mom," says Sally, who's struggling to support herself and her children after a divorce, "until she said, 'Here, at least let me pay for a cleaning lady.' "

The money, of course, is only a symbol.

The brownies, the homemade jellies, the whole frozen fish wrapped in newspaper my in-laws used to bring with them from Connecticut, the toilet paper and exotic tools my friend Bill's parents bring him, all carry a message: *Your parents still care about you.*

The AT&T calling card number sent for emergency use, the

suggestion to call collect, the paid-for plane tickets home, the cozy extra bedroom in the Florida condominium, the offer of "waffles the way you love them," are dispatches of the heart: *Keep in touch.*

In some families the unsolicited advice does not cease with age: "Why don't you do something with your hair?" "This couch would look so wonderful against that wall."

In others, the invidious comparisons continue to hit the shore in endless waves: "Would you believe that Mrs. Williams' daughter Rachel's husband Mark is an IBM vice-president at thirty-five?" ("Who, Mom? I never heard of any of them.")

Mothers and fathers, who see our faults clearly, are blind to our wrinkles, gray hair, bald spots, and varicose veins. The same message keeps making its way to kids with kids of their own: *You still need us.*

How silly can they get?

Just the same, I recently invited my mother to come to a talk I was giving. All right . . . I thought I'd show her that I'd finally mastered the proper use of silverware and could make my way to a podium without tripping. I thought she'd notice that I had great posture, that my slip wasn't showing, and that I no longer fiddled with my hair. I secretly hoped she might realize that her baby had become a grown woman.

I didn't get a chance to find out if she'd been properly impressed, however, for as we were leaving the room, a commotion erupted.

"Someone's stolen my pocketbook," a woman cried out.

My mother held up a leather bag she'd slung over her shoulder. "Isn't this yours?" she asked me.

I held up my own small clutch.

"You took my bag," the woman said, coming up behind us.

"My mother's a kleptomaniac," I said evilly, "but whenever I'm with her I always make her return the things she's taken."

"Linda . . ." warned my mother. I remembered that voice from childhood. It was the signal to stop dead in my tracks. "I'm sorry. I thought this was my daughter's bag," she explained to the woman. "I was afraid she'd forget it, so I was carrying it out for her."

"Look at me," I said to the woman, "and tell me you believe that ridiculous story."

"Linda . . . " warned my mother.
That'll teach her.
I hope.

W H E N   I   R E A C H E D
what is commonly called "middle
age," I noticed I'd gained a friend
I affectionately referred to as Five Extra Pounds. I tried not to mind
when her buddy, Three Extra Pounds, joined us and refused to
leave. To tell you the truth, I resented their decision to hang
around me day and night, but I couldn't seem to get rid of them.
You'd think by now I'd be able to accept their attachment to me,
but nothing seemed to help.

I tried scowling at skin-and-bone models in *Vogue*. I told
myself Madison Avenue was promoting self-dissatisfaction as a way
to make me spend money. I reassured myself that my husband and
friends liked how I look. I observed myself naked in the mirror and
noticed that the curve of my belly was actually aesthetically pleasing.

Then I gave up. I tried not to think about it.

Recently, however, I attended a week-long program at the
Option Institute. The Institute's founder, Barry Neil Kaufman, has
written a book called *To Love Is To Be Happy With*. One afternoon,
as a way of being happy with ourselves, he directed us to focus on
loving our bodies.

"Pick something you're judging and describe it," he said.

I chose my stomach, then watched in horror as a stream of
invective poured forth from my pen: "thick, unattractive, dumpy,
lumpy, over-the-hill, sedentary, piggy, sloppy, pointless, useless,
discounted, don't care about yourself, like my mother and aunts."

"What do you feel about this?" he asked.

I started in again: "disgust, disdain, dislike, hopelessness,
shame . . . " Then I stopped. Even I could see these words were
overkill, like using a machete to spread butter. My poor stomach

had done nothing to deserve this abuse. Where did these feelings come from?

I glanced back at what I'd written, stopping at, "like my mother and aunts." I remembered being a slim-hipped girl of sixteen. My mother must have been all of forty-five, but she and her sisters seemed old to me — too old to sit on the floor, or ride bikes, or laugh uproariously. They played Mah Jongg and wore girdles. As far as I could see, my mom had long ago given up on her looks and her marriage. She didn't have a paid job and soon lost interest in all her hobbies, whether she was making records for the blind, painting landscapes, or helping teach at Headstart. I didn't think my mother or my aunts had achieved much of anything.

I must have thought: *I won't grow up and be like them.* I must have thought: *I won't grow up and look like them.* Now that I, too, am "past my prime," when I catch a glimpse of my reflection in a store window, I see my mother and my Aunt Pearl and my Aunt Evelyn all jumbled up into me. My judgment of them has come full circle.

I'm holding it against myself.

I take some comfort from Paula Kaplan's book *Don't Blame Mother*.

"Daughters often believe that they want to avoid taking on their mothers' individual, personal characteristics," she writes. "But a little probing usually shows that what daughters really want to avoid is anything connected with women's devalued and limited position: her mother's weight doesn't fit the slender feminine mold; she gets no respect outside the home, she is intimidated by her husband; she has no skills that are appreciated in the public world."

These things not only bothered me, I think they bothered many women in my mother's generation. I was sixteen in the mid-fifties, and for all the golden glow of the "good old days," a woman's usefulness pretty much came to an end when her children were old enough to get along without her. My mother certainly didn't value herself as a mother, a housewife, or a volunteer, and neither did anyone else she knew, yet because she couldn't see any other roles open to her, she blamed herself. Afraid of someday finding myself in my mother's position, I blamed her, too. Neither one of us understood that her lack of status and power was a result of widespread cultural norms, not a personal defect.

I looked at her body and indicted her life: *pointless.*

I looked at her figure and judged her achievements: *useless.*

All the nights she cheered as I swam competitively for the Worcester Aqua-Maids, the car trip we took without my father to see all the historical landmarks between Boston and Miami, all the ingenuity she showed in making sure I got a good education, all her encouragement and faith in me: *discounted.*

I was afraid that if I approved of her, I'd end up like her.

I was afraid that if I didn't distance myself from her, I might become her.

Yet I can see that, even in the ways I'm not like her, my accomplishments rest on the foundation she gave me. With a generous heart, she did her best to prepare me for a life she knew would always be outside her grasp.

It's time to stand in front of the mirror with clear eyes.

Until I discard my judgments along with my clothes, I'll never make peace with how I look.

WHY DO OUR PARENTS loom larger than life long after we've outgrown other childish ways of looking at the world? I should have been able to see my folks as merely human long before this, but there was something in my response to them that gave them mythic proportions. Even as a grown woman, I felt a mixture of amazement and pride as their stories made their way to my door.

December 1988

I remember when my dad, in his eighties, had his picture on the front page of the Worcester newspaper, riding his bicycle down Route 9 in the midst of the winter's worst blizzard. In eighteen months, he survived six falls from his bicycle — including a collision with a car — and emerged with only a few bruises and a broken chain. The doctors informed him he had the blood profile of a young man, which he took as a personal triumph for his diet of cod liver oil and crushed wheat berries.

If my father's eccentricity was legendary, my mother was equally famous for her stubbornness. No, she would not watch her diet just because she had diabetes. No, she would not exercise just because the doctor insisted. At last, having moved to Florida without my dad, she had the apartment of her dreams. She was free from her husband's criticism and her children's demands. She had, late in life, decided to follow her own star and, no matter how much her family entreated, she was not about to be swayed by any of our arguments. I was in awe of her willfulness.

I suppose I believed my father would die undiminished, still chug-a-lugging cod liver oil straight from the bottle. The child in me envisioned my mother, strong-willed as ever, refusing to compromise even for death. Then, last spring, it became apparent my parents could not afford to live apart much longer. In November, my mother had a small stroke that left her physically unable to carry out her daily routine. As we children tried to come up with some solution, my father felt the last of his freedom ebbing away. Afraid to fly, he boarded a train and went to Boca Raton to take care of a wife he had not lived with for eighteen years.

By that time none of us could imagine them together.

My sister, my brother, and I tried to help my parents adjust to this new twist of fate. Susan and her husband spent weeks in Florida, straightening out our parents' financial affairs. Ken and his wife, Barbara, flew down to check on our folks' medical coverage and to see if their grandson, Sam, could coax them out of their despondency. We siblings kept in touch and tried to make a difference. Mostly, we acknowledged our helplessness.

"Listen," I said to my sister, "we have to keep in mind that this is the life they created. Dad could have let us find him a less expensive apartment here. You offered to put an addition on your house for Mom, but she said she wouldn't come north under any conditions. They made choices, and now they're living with them. We have to stop feeling guilty, as if there were something we could have done."

It wasn't only guilt we were coping with. It was something

less easy to identify, something that crept up without warning and clouded our perception of who we were. Surely, as adults, we possessed a new and unshakable maturity. But, no, my father's distress and my mother's vulnerability reverberated through our lives though we were thousands of miles away.

"I've been having this feeling that I'm not doing anything productive," my sister, Susan, confided to me one day. "I keep having the thought that what I'm doing with my life is not important, and then I realize I'm somehow taking on Mother's feelings as my own."

I murmured words of consolation, grateful I wasn't similarly affected by my parents' troubled reconciliation. Then this past week, a nerve in my neck began throbbing, throwing me off balance. As I lay awake one night, unable to sleep, I suddenly felt overwhelmed by grief. For a moment I forgot that eventually this pain would go away. I saw the end of my life, and it was the end of my mother's life as well. She was no longer gloriously willful, but weary and confused. Trapped by her body's weakness, she was forced to submit to her husband's hated control. My father, too, was no longer master of his destiny. Cut off from his friends and his usual routine, he was trapped in a strange apartment with a woman he did not respect. It had been only my illusion that my all-powerful parents would be able to resist the forces that squeeze us smaller and smaller through the years.

For better or worse, my parents are together again, and all their children's good intentions cannot bring them contentment nor save them from facing the consequences at the end of their lives. Once upon a time they protected us from all the evil in the world, but they were mighty then only because we were small and desperately needed to believe that they could vanquish our greatest fears.

Those days are gone.

So the generations pass. Our parents become merely human. The world empties of protection. I relinquish the vision of my mother as an obstinate Joan of Arc. I release the father who once stood taller than Paul Bunyan. We children must practice the art of accepting what we cannot control.

And not only for our parents' sake.

April 1989

MY MOTHER CAN STILL hurt my feelings.

No, that's not right. My mother says things — with no harmful intent, but without thinking how they sound — and I turn her words into little daggers and stick myself with them. I hurt my own feelings, but that insight doesn't help all that much. I still hurt.

For example, my mother up came up from Florida last month to visit my sister, my brother, and me. I was looking forward to making my mother's visit a pleasant break from the tension between her and my dad, though I should have foreseen that my expectations always set me up for disappointment.

"I'll pick you up at the airport on Wednesday," I told her on the phone. "You'll stay with us until Saturday when everyone's coming here for dinner. Then you'll go home with Susan."

"I want to see Sam," she said. Sam is my brother's son.

"Mom, Sam's in daycare during the week. You'll see him Saturday."

"But I want to see *Sam*," she repeated.

"Well, you can't."

"You mean I don't get to see *anybody* until Saturday?" she asked.

My excitement turned to ashes in my mouth. "Mom, you'll see my family. Then in three days you'll see everyone else."

"All right," she said. "I'm looking forward to seeing you."

Now why would I choose to latch on to the sentence about not being *anybody*, instead of accepting that I'm someone my mother's looking forward to seeing? I don't know the answer, but I felt exhausted, as if I'd been having this conversation for half a century. I was close to tears when the phone rang.

"Linda, it's Susan," said my sister who lives thirty miles away with her husband in Waltham. "Pierce was afraid I'd hurt your feelings, but I had to call. I've been thinking about your plan to have Mom stay with you for the first few days of her visit. I think you'll have a hard time. If you like, you can drive her to our house the morning after she arrives, and then Pierce and I will bring her back to your place for dinner on Saturday night."

I don't know why I've been blessed with a brother-in-law who's worried about hurting my feelings. Or with a sister who can say, without disapproval, "I think you'll have a hard time." It hasn't always been this way. Maybe that's why it's important for me to say publicly how much it means to me to have my sister not only accept me, but actually care enough to try to help. It's a small miracle, as if someone had come and thrown away our family's rules when I wasn't looking.

I was brought up to believe that family members were the only people who told you the truth. This sounded great in principle. In practice, it meant they were the ones who always told you the bad news. Relatives were the ones who let you know how terrible you looked and how badly you acted, who never forgot a thing you'd done wrong. The way I was raised, politeness was only for company.

We also lived by the scarcity principle. For some reason I never understood, there could be only one smart or pretty or successful child in a family. Since someone was always falling short by comparison, siblings and cousins fought for the spotlight, making themselves look good by putting one another down. To the day we die, my cousin Margie will be dumb because I'm smart, and I'll be plain because she's pretty. In my family, there could only be one winner per category.

So I wouldn't have blamed Susan if she'd informed me that this was just one more instance of her having to do more than her share because of my oversensitivity, or if she'd cast herself as the only daughter my mother could count on. I wouldn't have been surprised to find my own judgments — *you're acting like a child; you're making a fuss over nothing* — echoed in her words.

Yet Susan wasn't choosing sides or making me wrong. She wasn't trying to straighten me out or change me. She could acknowledge that I loved my mother, too, no matter how awkwardly, and she wanted my mother's visit to go well for all of us. A wave of relief swept over me, followed by gratitude. There is no greater gift Susan could have given me than to allow me all my imperfections.

The visit wasn't effortless — life never is — but Susan's support carried me over the rough parts. I felt soothed by her concern. I felt safe, and that enabled me to notice that the feelings my mother stirs up in me are part of the baggage I always carry around. Not only did I enjoy myself, I even stopped trying to measure which of her children my mother preferred.

At the end of her visit, I drove my mother to the airport. We were in the car, reviewing everything that had happened during her visit: "I picked you up at the airport on Wednesday, and the next morning I took you to Susan's," I said.

"Why did you do that?" she asked.

"You didn't want to spend three days at my house," I reminded her. "You didn't want to have to wait until Saturday to see everybody."

"I never said that," she insisted.

I looked over at her. No question, she meant it.

"If you say so," I said and squeezed her hand.

It no longer hurt.

October 1989

MY HUSBAND, JACK, and I had a difference of opinion. On his way back from visiting his mother in Florida, he wanted to change planes in Philadelphia so he could see our daughter Laura and her fiancé. I tried to reroute him.

"Hon, the kids were just here, and we're going to visit them in April," I said. "You're putting them under pressure by expecting them to drive all the way out to the airport to see you."

"If they don't want me to come, they can tell me," he said.

I didn't know what to say next. It didn't bother him that our daughters would never hurt his feelings by telling him the trip to the airport was an awfully long drive for a ten-minute visit. Unlike me, he's comfortable asking for anything. What's more, I wasn't sure I wanted to convert him to my point of view. It didn't seem to be working out that well for me. Maybe he's right, and it's better to err on the side of being over-present in your kids' lives.

My husband comes from a structured family. No matter how

strained relations are, he calls home every Sunday night. In contrast, I don't call home unless there's something particular to convey. Still, every time I call, my dad seems amazed to hear from me. He acts as if I'm calling from another planet. He checks that it's the best time for cheap phone rates. He confirms that nothing terrible has happened. Then he hangs up. Heaven forbid I should waste my money "chatting" with him.

My in-laws were attentive children all their lives; they expect as much from their son. My parents were equally devoted to their folks, but as far as I can tell, they don't expect a thing from their kids, not even a phone call on their birthdays. They act as if the worst sin parents can commit is imposing on their children. When I was younger, I preferred my parents' philosophy of voluntary association.

Now I'm not so sure.

After my last breakthrough, I was looking forward to my mother's next visit, but this time, soon after she arrived, she informed me that she really hadn't wanted to come, that she would never have left Florida if my brother's wife hadn't just had a baby girl. I nodded, knowing how much she hates cold weather and how little she likes travel. I even thought I understood her motives. It made her feel less guilty about "imposing" on her children if she appeared to arrive unwillingly. I tried to rise above my ego, to stop feeling terrible about the fact that she hadn't wanted to see me, but I kept getting sadder. I had to say something.

"Why would you tell me you don't want to spend time with me?" I asked.

"Why are you so upset? You always say you don't want to come to Florida, and I don't get upset," she replied.

"Mom, I say I don't want to come and I don't come, but I don't show up on your doorstep announcing that I don't want to be there."

"But I *didn't* want to come," she insisted. "Should I lie?"

We didn't resolve anything on this trip. In fact, she caught such a bad cold that it seemed inadvisable for her to even hold her grandchild. With Sarah out of bounds, she left early. Eventually word came back through the grapevine: My mother's visit had been a "disaster."

I don't take these things lying down. I called my sister.

"It's a blind spot the two of you have," Susan said. "Mom isn't confident you really love her, and you're not confident that she really loves you. That's what all your arguments boil down to."

I thought about that for a while. Then I called my mother.

"Mom," I said after a few minutes of small talk, "first, your visit wasn't a disaster in my book. Growing up in our family, if one little thing went wrong, everything was ruined, but the way I look at it, everyone enjoyed having you here, and you and I got along great except for our one disagreement. I wasn't angry with you, either. I was hurt. I want you to *want* to be with me."

My mother didn't soften, but a week later she called me back.

"I always hold back for fear of being too demanding," she said, "but I can see how you could take that as rejection, which I don't intend. When Jack comes to Florida to see his mother, I'm going to visit the two of them this time instead of feeling I'd be in the way. Is that all right?"

Who besides someone raised in my family would think it wouldn't be all right?

So my husband will stop in Philly to see our daughter, with my blessings. When I told Laura to feel free to discourage him from coming, she acted as if I were crazy. How strange that I couldn't anticipate that she'd be delighted that her father was rerouting his trip in order to spend a few minutes in her company.

My mother's change of heart has made me see that it's all right to offer your kids more of yourself than you think they could possibly want and allow them to set the limits.

Isn't it ironic? In challenging my mother's way of thinking, I've changed my own.

October 1990

"HOW DOES YOUR MOTHER feel about appearing in your column?" an older woman asked me at the end of a talk.

I could feel the audience holding its breath, waiting for my answer. They identified with my mother.

I could see comic-strip balloons rising over their heads: *How could you put in the newspaper that you felt anxious about an upcoming visit from your mother? Or confess that your mother could still hurt your feelings? How could you reveal the conflicts in your relationship so openly?*

For years my readers have watched me struggle with the difficulties of being my mother's daughter, wondering, I suppose, what I thought I was accomplishing by holding our collisions up to the light.

Now they could ask me what was really on their minds: *How could you do such a thing to your mom?*

I would have asked that same question back when I thought I had a clear picture of the "ideal" mother-child relationship. I played the role of loving daughter most of my life, often with grim compliance, trying to the best of my ability to keep my disagreeable feelings from showing. I heaved a sigh of relief when my performance was over, but every time my mother and I parted, I felt sad and guilty about what I considered my hardness of heart. I wasn't fooling anyone, including my mom who often confided in my sister. She knew I was only going through the motions.

A lot of things began to make sense when I learned that I was born at an especially difficult time in her marriage. I stopped feeling demeaned by her constant stream of advice when she explained to me that she was bossy because she felt the best she had to offer as a mother were suggestions for her children's improvement. I never thought my mother — whose byword when I was growing up was, "Take me or leave me; this is the way I am" — could change at this stage of the game, but I was wrong. It just took time.

You have to understand: Whenever I wrote about my mother, I shared my rough drafts with her and with my siblings, and made whatever changes were necessary to tell the truth of their experience as well as my own. My mother and I were exquisitely vulnerable to one another, and so it hurt sometimes to find that something we'd said or done had been misunderstood. When that happened, we expressed our feelings as honestly as we could and tried to see the situation from one another's point of view. It wasn't easy, or painless, or always successful. Still, I felt it was a vast improvement over the game of make-believe we'd once played.

In that respect, this column has been a gift, for it has offered us the opportunity to work through the pain instead of burying it. My mother has allowed me to write about how far our family was from ideal because each time a troublesome issue came up, we dealt with it by moving to another level of understanding. In the process I think I came a long way in replacing my child's view of my mother with a more realistic and appreciative one.

I haven't shared this particular column with my mother, but I think she'd agree with that assessment. She never asked me *not* to write about what was going on between us. I think she wanted others to learn from our experience what we were learning the hard way: how to dismantle the barriers to loving one another. I think she shared my feeling that we were not the only mother and daughter in the world struggling to connect.

Our honest exchanges did more than clear the air between us. I changed and so did she. We learned that we didn't have to settle for anything less than genuine warmth between us. During her last visit, after I explained that I wanted her to let me put myself out for her, she actually relented and agreed to go along with whatever I suggested.

"This was the nicest time I've ever had," she said before she left.

I called her at the beginning of this month to tell her I was making plans to come to Florida. Her doctors had discovered a potentially life-threatening medical problem and had scheduled an exploratory operation in a few weeks.

"You don't have to go to all that bother," she said, dismissing my offer. In times past, I would have concluded that she took no pleasure from my company, but I've learned that she pushes me away because she feels she doesn't deserve attention. She doesn't want her children acting out of a sense of duty. To melt the barrier between us, all I had to do was assure her that I truly wanted to be with her.

"Mom," I said softly, but firmly, "I want to drive you to the hospital and be with you until you go into the operating room. I want to be there when you wake up and keep you company while you're recuperating. Then I'll bring you home and get everything in the apartment in order before I leave you with Dad. It's no problem for me. I can write from anywhere. I want to go through this with you."

"That would be nice," she said in the child's voice she'd taken to using at times of stress. "I love you."

"I love you too, Mom," I said with a whole heart. I was grateful that I had worked through my petty grievances and had stopped reading rejection into everything she said or did. I could feel waves of warmth crossing miles of telephone wire. I hung up the phone.

Two hours later, I lay me down to sleep. Before I woke, my mother passed away of a sudden and silent heart attack in the early hours of the morning.

She died before I woke . . . but, thank God, not until we'd made peace with one another.

December 1994

I TOOK PART IN A guided visualization last week. As my friend Nancy put on a tape, I closed my eyes, took a few deep breaths, and let myself imagine that I stood in a wide, sunlit meadow. The voice on the tape instructed us to visualize several paths leading from the meadow into the woods, each path leading to a person with whom we had unfinished business. We were to follow one until we came face-to-face with the person we were seeking.

I mentally recreated a familiar path from our land in Vermont, a rutted incline leading down to a stream. I was expecting to visualize my husband, so I was shocked to find my mother sitting on a flat stone bench next to the stream. I was so shocked that I turned my image around and went back to the meadow. This time I chose a different path, but somehow it led me back to the same pool of water, and there was my mother, still patiently waiting, wrapped in a shroud of sadness.

Though my eyes were already shut, I closed a second pair in my mind, hoping to dislodge her, but when I opened them again, my mother was still there, eyes downcast, preoccupied, hardly aware of me.

I sat down beside her. *I thought I resolved my relationship with you before you died,* I said silently. *What is there left to say? What is this all about?* Suddenly my eyes filled with tears. I knew why she'd come into my mind.

"I'm sorry," I whispered, putting my imagined hand on hers. "Oh, Mom, I owe you an apology."

Every once in a while an experience of this sort reminds me how powerful the unconscious is. We ignore and underestimate the nonrational aspects of our personality, pretending we're sensible creatures who always have a reason for our actions, even if we have to make one up on the spot. We rarely quiet the chatter inside long enough for the images and themes buried within us to break through to ordinary reality. But having opened myself up to a message from my unconscious, information that I'd tucked away was suddenly accessible. I could no longer manage to ignore something that had crossed my mind months ago.

My mother probably had Adult Attention Deficit Disorder.

I remember the night my husband, who is a psychiatrist, told me he had an explanation for my forgetfulness, my distractibility, and my constant struggle to keep chaos within manageable limits. He gave my symptoms a name — Adult ADD — and that enabled me to get a hold on "habits" of mind I'd thought were out of my control. I saw a specialist in the field, tried and rejected two medications, then decided to build structures into my daily life that would help me function with more clarity.

As I became aware of my own behavior patterns, I recognized in me traits I'd disliked in my mother. At last I understood that they were involuntary, caused not by a lack of love or an indifference to others' needs, but by a metabolic abnormality in our brains. This new knowledge brought into question judgments I'd made as a child.

I used to think my mother was bored with me when her mind

wandered in the middle of our conversations. I thought she didn't care about my feelings when she kept the house so messy I was reluctant to invite friends over. I thought she was torturing me when she put off doing things until the last minute. I thought her chronic lateness was her way of expressing anger at my dependence on her. I made up an entire mythology of blame because I was totally unaware of what my mother was going through, and I carried it, like an unopened suitcase, into adulthood.

At times, the thought that my mother might have had ADD flashed across my mind, but I would instantly move on. This visualization gave me another chance to review the past and resolve this issue with my mom.

How could I have had unfinished business with my mother and not have known it? The answer is, I think, that we all possess an inner wisdom that can help us — but only if we're willing to open ourselves to it. This is not the first time my mind, in dreams or in guided visualizations, has brought up spontaneous images that led me to a greater understanding of the meaning of my life.

Poet Robert Frost wrote, "We dance around in a ring and suppose . . . But the secret sits in the middle and knows."

This is the real miracle of our being, that each of us possesses an intuitive inner process that can help us identify what is unfolding at the deepest levels of our psyches. It is our personal link with the creative principle that pervades the universe. Every time I have opened myself to the part of me that speaks in symbols and images, it has led me beyond the limitations of my own understanding toward a reconciliation, not only of the real and the possible, but between the living and the dead.

My Father's Daughter

January 1983

MY FATHER IS DOWN in the dumps.

Well, not exactly. To be more accurate, at this very moment my father is probably down in one of the six dumpsters in his apartment complex, hauling out a mess of treasures you wouldn't believe: toys, electrical appliances, magazines and books, pots and dishes, a Persian rug, bookcases, lamps, and even a small black-and-white television set.

"It's like a flea market," he tells me, extending a bright red bow tie he retrieved after the holidays. "These dumpsters are like having a garden. When I go out, I never know what I'll find." My dad sits down on a leather swivel chair. "This chair will outlive me," he continues.

I don't have to ask where the chair came from. It came from the same place as the wicker rocker, the yellow lamp, the blender, and the painting over the couch. Given his twice daily excursions to the dumpsters, it's a wonder my dad's apartment has room for my dad.

"I know people who will take practically anything," my father boasts. A fence would envy his ability to turn over merchandise quickly. "I have a friend named Rocky who owns a house, and a friend George who takes stuff to his mother. Just the other day I found a hand-knit Irish sweater worth at least fifty dollars. Rocky gave it to his girlfriend." My dad points to a box in the corner. "You like *Cosmo*? I've got the whole year there."

If you think this is the hobby of a bored old man, desperate to fill the hours of his seventy-eighth year, you're wrong, My father's never been bored, never pursued any interest half-heartedly. A hobby? The very word is an insult. Scavenging is his source of excitement, his daily adventure, his all-consuming passion, an art form that requires timing and perseverance.

Take newspapers. He reads *The Wall Street Journal*, *The New York Times*, and the *Boston Globe* — a few days late, but for free.

"If I miss a newspaper," he explains with the confidence of an old hand, "there are five more dumpsters to go." He points to his plaid shirt. "I've given away at least fifty shirts in perfect condition. You think your husband would wear this?"

My father has a theory about why such treasures make their way to him. "People have no other alternative when they leave. The people in these buildings are young professionals moving up. They move like gypsies, and I'm sure they think it would be an insult to offer their possessions to anyone. I think they still cherish them because they place them so carefully in the dumpsters. I've found innumerable blankets and puffs, most of them clean and carefully folded. There are seventy-two apartments, and every one of them has a garbage disposal, so there's no food on anything I find," he says, taking note of my suspicious demeanor. "I suppose you couldn't use the one-volume edition of the *Illustrated World Encyclopedia?*"

My father is a big-game hunter, passing on the secrets by which he stalks his prey. "Anything I want, all I have to do is wait a minute," he says proudly. "I walk by in the morning. That's when people drop stuff off on their way to work. Then I go by in the afternoon, when the women have finished their housework. I'm always surprised to see what's turned up. I don't go into closed bags. I just take what's visible.

"It's gotten to the point where if it isn't in absolutely perfect condition, I won't even touch it. I figure if the appliances don't work, I'll throw them back. You know what? They work. There's a young couple here, newly married, getting a divorce. They're throwing out all their wedding presents. You want towels from Lord and Taylor?

"Listen," he says, before I leave. "I take orders. I can get you all the medical books and journals you could ever want, ironing boards, kitchen chairs, barbecue grills used just a few times. I find at least one mirror a week. Too bad you have a king-size bed. I found brand new designer double sheets still in their wrapping, with 'your so special' misspelled all over them. I mailed them to your brother."

We hug. I carry an armful of gifts to my car.

"Too bad you live in Marblehead," my dad says sympathetically, as I back the car out from the shadow of a big blue dumpster. "Slim pickings. I bet they wrap everything in plastic bags up there."

They do.

I feel deprived all the way home.

October 1984

WE LEARN AS CHILDREN, in or out of Sunday school, that "it's better to give than to receive." This isn't exclusively a woman's burden, this obligation to give unstintingly of time and energy. Men also feel obligated to provide their families with the necessities and the luxuries of existence. All our heroes and heroines have generous hearts. Our villains are "stingy," "tight-fisted," "miserly," and "mean."

We don't have any words, however, for those who give but are unable to take. What happens in a relationship when the recipient is denied the chance to reciprocate?

That was my experience, growing up as the child of a self-educated Russian immigrant who took pride in giving his children the advantages he never had. He barely noticed when I brought home glowing report cards. The quarters I saved when finances were tight were dismissed out-of-hand. My father gave away every birthday present I ever gave him. When he was ill, he disappeared rather than accept his family's solicitude.

He never seemed to need anyone or anything.

Eventually, I came to admire my father's self-sufficiency. I thought it was admirable not to need the affection I myself craved and to be able to depend entirely upon yourself. When my father insisted his children were under no obligation to him, mere arrows to his bow, I should have been relieved.

Why have I found it so difficult to fly away?

I've begun to think about my dad in a new light since reading the book *Invisible Loyalties* by Ivan Boszormenyi-Nagy and Geraldine Spark. These two psychiatrists put forth a theory of family justice that requires a balance of giving and taking between the generations. Children, it seems, cannot escape feeling an obligation to their parents. Deprived of a chance to discharge that debt, they experience guilt and feelings of inadequacy.

It struck me that some parents have a talent: They know how to let their children make them happy. They're able to take pleasure in their kids, feeling amply repaid by a kind remark, an extra effort, or a tension-relieving joke. They tell their sons and daughters how much they're appreciated, express delight in the way one cares for the dog or another unpacks the groceries. By their ability to enjoy the ways children contribute to the well-being of a family, such parents demonstrate how gratifying it can be to give *and* take.

I've tried to be that kind of parent myself, but my father had no such aspirations. I think he resisted acknowledging any kindness toward him because he couldn't bear the thought of being under obligation. My father kept a careful accounting that left others forever in his debt, but he clearly wanted nothing back from his children — in the present or in the future. Perhaps he wanted to spare us the feelings of parental responsibility that had derailed his own youthful independence. I suspect he'd been given so little in his lifetime, and had learned to live with that at such a cost, that he couldn't even consider the possibility that his children might be a source of gratification.

My father often told us the folk tale of the eagle carrying her three babies across the sea:

> *"Will you carry me when I grow old?" the mother asks.*
> *When the first two reply, "Yes," she drops them into the water.*
> *The third eaglet declares that, when he grows up, he will carry his own children instead. This is the only one the mother allows to live.*

I always hated that story. Why couldn't the mother have let the good will of her first two lighten her burden? I understood the point my father was making, but why did loving your own children mean you had to totally forsake your parents?

On bad days, I think the tale demonstrates that those who cannot accept love in return deal out a kind of death to their offspring, but at other times I understand that, for the last little eaglet, survival meant accepting his mother's terms. He learned, as I am slowly learning myself, that some accounts can be settled only by letting go of ledgers and accepting, at last, that sometimes we must take and take and only be grateful, no matter how painful it may be.

FAMILY PUZZLES

EVERY MORNING IN MY kitchen, the scene repeats itself.

With my left hand, I reach for a slice of orange. With my right, I grasp a pint bottle of pure Norwegian cod liver oil. I take a swig of the thick golden liquid, letting it slide down my throat. I suck on the orange, chewing on the pulp until my mouth feels normal again. Then I heave a deep sigh of relief, and ask myself the usual question:

Why am I drinking cod liver oil?

Am I a follower of some bizarre food cultist? Am I under the influence of someone with the secret of eternal youth? Have I been brainwashed into thinking this will keep me supple and healthy?

Yes, yes, and yes.

The guru is my dad, and for as far back as I can remember he's been trying to convert everyone to his fishy regimen.

My father frequented health food stores back in the days when the only people in them were old or sick. In the 1950s, he was the only person in the city of Worcester who set off for work on a bicycle. In his relentless pursuit of physical fitness, he'd climb ten flights of stairs in a public building and meet the rest of us at the top. I accompanied him once and realized what he really meant by "climb": He crawled up the empty stairway on his hands and feet. I was puffing right behind him.

"Might as well strengthen the upper body," he explained, pitying the puny folk who rode in cars and elevators. He was ahead of his time. The whole world was his health club.

He matched my mother.

I remember how embarrassed I was by her habit of talking to strangers. My mother made friends on buses, in movie theaters, and in elevators, and she didn't always restrict herself to suitable women of the same age. As a child, going into the water at the beach was always a risk. You never knew who you'd find on her blanket when you came out. Even driving in the car wasn't safe. One time, traveling on Cape Cod, we ending up chatting with the military guards who'd whistled at us from the gates at Camp Edwards.

I thought responding to strangers was unmotherly, undignified, and totally unsuitable for a relative of mine. Now I do it myself.

And embarrass my children.

When did I turn into a crackpot chip-off-the-old-block? When did I discover that my parents' most grievous faults had turned into their most appealing virtues?

The day I noticed how much fun they were having.

I grew up painfully aware that my folks were unconventional. My father was always playing practical jokes and "showing off" at family gatherings. He sunbathed in the nude on the roof of his office building. I wanted to die. My mother took oil-painting classes and transcribed books into Braille instead of washing dishes and making beds like other mothers. What had I ever done to deserve such humiliation? They never gave me a bedtime or a curfew, or checked up on whether I'd done my homework. If they didn't want to act like parents, I asked myself, why did they have children?

When I grew up, my only ambition was to be normal — even if it killed me. And it almost did. There I was, eating peanut-butter-and-jelly sandwiches while my father swallowed raw eggs, whipped up wheat berry frappes, and exercised constantly by swiveling on a rotating disc whenever he watched TV or talked on the phone. At seventy-four, he was playing singles tennis three times a week — and winning — while I grew more sedentary by the minute. My mother seemed to be growing younger, too. At sixty-five, she had breast reduction surgery in spite of her children's objections. While I dutifully struggled to be the perfect wife and mother, I couldn't help but notice that the more my parents followed their own impulses, the happier and more relaxed they seemed.

I've been getting more peculiar ever since.

In addition to chug-a-lugging cod liver oil and talking to strangers, I shower with the dog. I cook everything on high. On the Fourth of July, I'm the only adult who wears a costume in our neighborhood parade. To my surprise, I often find that I'm doing exactly what I want to do. I know these are only mildly unusual forms of behavior, not the three-ring circus my parents held up as a standard, but remember, I'm just getting the hang of this.

I have a few more decades to hit my stride.

June 1988

MY HUSBAND AND I went to see "Les Misérables" at the Shubert as our Christmas gift to one another. We bought the tape for our cars. I've played the songs so many times, I hear the music playing in my head. The play was so satisfying that we went to see it again for our anniversary.

It brought back memories of my childhood.

Not the plot, mind you, but the thrill of being in the audience is something I learned as a child. My love of theater is one of the most valuable gifts my father ever gave me. When his father died, his mother went to work as a barber and he left school at fourteen to work in a factory. Yet, in spite of his lack of a formal education, my father was a man of many passions and one of them was the stage.

Back in the fifties, my dad, my mother, and I would make the hour drive to Boston. Dressed to the teeth, we'd mingle with the elegant folk in the lobby. We might have been poor and living in a four-family house in a run-down neighborhood, but we sat in the orchestra, an usher having led us down the aisle as if we were royalty. At a signal the music would begin to flutter like the butterflies in my stomach, the house lights would dim, and the play would begin.

My dad never quite got the knack of sitting back and letting things happen. He'd begin talking as soon as the actors did.

"See that," he'd say, poking me in the side. "Those are real people on stage." Ten minutes later he'd repeat himself in case I'd missed it. "Those are human beings right in front of us," he'd whisper loud enough to be heard in the balcony. "This isn't fake like a movie." His comments became as much a part of my experience as eavesdropping at intermission or watching beautiful women touch up their make-up in the bathroom.

I recall the construction of a house on stage during "Plain and Fancy," a musical about the Amish, along with my father's accompanying narration. A little voice repeats his words in my head to this day. "Ah," it said as I watched the barricades in "Les Miserables" revolve, "now that's a real special effect, not some cheap camera trick."

The years went by. When I met the man I later married and

found out he also liked taking me to plays, I was pleased to pass this information on to my dad. I thought he'd be impressed.

"What kind of tickets does he get?" my father asked.

"We sit in the balcony," I said.

A look came over my father's face, the one he reserved for second-rate things like movies. "I knew he was a cheapskate," he said.

Actually I was thrilled to hear it. My father had indulged in enough extravagant gestures to last me for a lifetime. I was tired of worrying about just when we'd be going to the poorhouse. I wanted someone a little more sensible with money, but as it turned out, seeing "Evita" from the last balcony and "Sweeney Todd" from the outfield, convinced my husband and me that my dad had been right. The thrill of a live performance requires an intimate connection between actors and audience.

For that, you need seats up front.

I wish my husband and I could take my dad to "Les Misérables" on Father's Day and surprise him with orchestra seats, but he'd never accept. My desire to give him something of value is just the remains of an enduring impulse to make him take something from me so I'll feel I contribute something to our relationship.

Someone else's child could just tell him in words, but when we speak on the phone, my father talks. I never get a word in edgewise. Over the years, since I know he reads it faithfully, this column has become my only way of communicating with him at length, so here goes:

After all these years, Dad, the cheapskate and I bought orchestra seats at a play just as elaborate as the ones you took me to when I was a child. Jack and I sat up front, and all the old excitement you used to generate was still there for me, filling my head with wonder and amazement. I remember the good times with great affection. I love you. Happy Father's Day.

MOMENTS BEFORE our daughter Laura's wedding ceremony, I noticed that my father was missing. I was standing in front of the church when the rest of my family arrived.

"Dad's sick," my mom whispered. Then the ceremony began.

Two years ago when he didn't come to my brother's rehearsal dinner, I thought my father's self-esteem so hinged on picking up the bill that he couldn't tolerate eating at my brother Ken's expense, but who knows? My father does not, will not, has never explained himself. Still, Dad attended Ken's wedding. He'd said that "if he were still alive," he'd make Laura's wedding, too. But Saturday, when relatives arrived to pick him up, he declined their offer of a ride.

On Sunday, when the last guest had gone, I called him.

"Dad, how are you feeling?" I asked.

"You didn't have to bother calling," he replied. "I wasn't going to tell anyone I was sick, but when they came here, what could I do? You're busy. Don't let me keep you. Good-bye."

"Dad, wait," I said. "I wanted to let you know that you don't have to miss the wedding just because you couldn't come. We had a videotape made, and when it's ready, I'll show it to you."

"Don't bother," he said. His tone of voice indicated there was no chance of changing his mind. "Why go to all the work of coming to Worcester? I don't want anyone to put themselves out for me. Just leave me alone." He began to laugh. "Okay? Good-bye."

I should have let it go. I'd called. I'd offered to show him the video. What more could a daughter do for a stubborn old man? I was bone-weary, but not too tired to call my sister.

"Susan," I asked, "is anything actually wrong with Dad?"

"Well, tomorrow's Mom's seventy-fifth birthday, and I thought Pierce and I would drive in to Worcester to celebrate with her and dad. We'll check on him. Ken's coming, but you're exhausted. Why don't you stay home and recuperate from the wedding?"

Why didn't I? My father is as constant as the North Star. Why did I keep thinking this time it would be different? The wedding had been a joyous occasion from start to finish. I knew that because I could feel the pleasure of it deep inside me. Why didn't I stick with that feeling? What did I want from my father?

At another, even more dangerous, level of thinking, what did I think I could do for him? Why did I persist in trying to be a good daughter? I imagined he was disappointed to miss his grand-daughter's wedding, but the fact is that my father chooses to withdraw from people when he's ill, even to the extent of not telling anyone that he's entering a hospital for treatment. I know this about him. Why couldn't I leave him alone?

Longing for family tripped me up. Then fatigue administered the finishing blow. If I'd been my own best friend, I'd never have let myself get in the car.

The next day Susan and her husband, Pierce, drove me into Worcester with them. In my pocketbook were wedding photographs taken by various family members, which I'd had developed in a rush. When I arrived at my father's apartment, he was as cantankerous as ever. His step was firm, his voice was strong. I thought of my mother-in-law who'd flown up for the wedding from Florida at eighty-six. She'd needed a cane and an attendant to make it to the church, but she'd come. Then I let it go. If Dad hadn't felt well enough to go to the wedding, it was his call.

"Let me show you the photographs," I said, moving to sit beside him. He got up and began fiddling with things in the kitchen.

"That means no," my sister said.

"Dad, I really don't understand," I said. "Will you just tell me why you don't want to look at the wedding pictures?"

He turned. The expression on his face looked like pure hatred to me, but maybe it was only simple annoyance. I was in no condition to judge. Who ever knows what another person feels?

"Because I'm S-I-C-K," he spelled out in a voice so harsh it chilled the air-conditioned room.

I felt ashamed to have bothered him. As if I'd done something wrong, was wrong, would *always* be wrong. I felt an enormous sorrow, as if no one had ever loved me or ever would. I felt ten years old, and a child's voice was asking, "Why did you bring me here again?"

I sat quietly and said little, trying not to show emotion, trying not to feel any. My weariness hardened into cement. Like a robot, I finished out the evening.

The next day I went to see my friend Kaiya. I lay on her massage table. She kneaded the knots in my neck and listened to the whole sad story.

"No matter how hard I try, I can't seem to learn," I said.

"You have to surrender, Linda," she said. "Your dad is your dad. You have to accept him exactly as he is and give up everything you wish he were or want him to be. Just let all that go."

She's right, you know.

So I surrender, Dad.

I won't bother you again.

November 1988

I JUST FINISHED TALKING to my dad on the phone.

Surprised? I know I vowed never to talk to him again. I wrote that I'd never bother him again, but I didn't mean I'd cut him out of my life. I meant I'd stop burdening him with the expectations in my heart.

The day after my daughter's wedding, I'd come home so furious at my dad that I'd picked a fight with my husband and stormed off to sleep in the guest room. The next morning, all the angry words I'd thrown at Jack the night before were still echoing in the house like a script from my childhood, acted out in a flash of red-hot anger.

I sat down to write as a way of understanding what ancient kindling had been ignited inside me. By the time I reached the last sentence, I felt centered again. My father was back to human scale, a person with hurts inflicted by his own parents.

I was safely an adult again.

I could have tossed that column away, but when I took this job, I committed myself to the truth. Relationships require a whole person, even the relationship between writer and reader. My public persona is no better and no worse than I am myself, and that morning the woman who is also a columnist had stumbled into a small hole in time and really hurt herself.

Once I decided to publish that column, I had to acknowledge that my act would have consequences. I called my brother and read him what I'd written. Ken was both in sympathy with me and surprised at my immaturity — no easy combination. On Thursday morning, he drove to Worcester with Sam, his year-old son, to be there when my dad read the paper.

Before it appeared, I also read it to my sister.

"How do you feel about the column?" I asked, bracing myself.

"Linda, I've learned that I don't have to have a reaction to everything," she replied. "This is between you and Dad. I don't have to take a position."

I'm more grateful for my siblings' support than I can say, especially since our friendship hasn't come easily. I come from a family where cutting off contact is so commonplace that, at one time or another, everyone in my family wasn't speaking to somebody. We'd stop talking to relatives for years because of something they'd said to someone else. So it was a kind of miracle that my siblings weren't taking sides. They seemed to understand that I was doing the best I could.

A hurtful day. An upsurge of anger. A momentary cry of pain. All that could have turned into a permanent state of warfare if my sister and brother had attacked me, or if I'd buried those feelings, thereby preserving their bitterness.

Instead, in writing them down, I let them go.

In her wonderful book *Writing Down the Bones*, Natalie Goldberg says, "At the moment you write something down you are free because you are not fighting those things inside. You have accepted them, become one with them."

But, I can testify, not forever.

That's the amazing part. Writing thoughts and feelings down makes them real, yes, but it doesn't make them final. As Natalie Goldberg puts it, words help you to penetrate your life and become sane, and they do that because naming your emotions is like catching a wave and riding it to shore. You're afraid, you're exhilarated, you're on solid ground at last. As the moment flows through you, you step out of your frozen self and see that you are not only that moment, that expressing your feelings is a process that leads to another place.

Of course, I can afford to be philosophical. I didn't open the paper and find myself skewered. You want to know how my dad felt?

The truth is I'll never know that any more than I'll know how he felt when, as a teen-ager, I began to walk out the door on him before he could walk out on me. My dad and I know this dance well from lots of practice. Something he says or does leads to an explosive outburst on my part, followed by our mutual withdrawal, which is eventually ended by a gesture from me. I used to fill that dance with pain until I realized there was a pattern I could count on that always ended in a truce.

I continued to send my father copies of the weekly letters I sent my daughters. He continued to mail me clippings. When I finally called him on the phone, he acted as if nothing had happened. Whatever bond there is between us seems to be strong enough to withstand the assault of my anger and the force of his pride.

I grew up believing my father had no feelings, but I know better now. I see at last that his willingness to reconnect is one of the facets of his love.

_____

September 1992

I STEPPED OUT OF THE shower, wrapped in a towel, and caught sight of myself in a mirror. The sight of that skimpy towel hanging on for dear life reminded me of the most mortifying day of my life.

I was fifteen. I'd invited friends over, important girls from a high school sorority I desperately wanted to join. We were talking in my living room when my father appeared at the door. Teen-agers are reluctant to have their parents undergo their friends' scrutiny under the most favorable circumstances, but this was ridiculous. My father had just taken a shower. Dripping wet, he was wearing nothing but a towel.

"Bill, get out of there!" I can still hear my mother's voice following his detour through the living room.

"Dorothy," he said, pausing for maximum effect, "you don't want Linda's friends to think her father never bathes, do you?"

That moment is as vivid in my memory as the day it happened. I can smile now at how outrageous my dad was, though at the time I was sure I'd been sired by a madman. My father had a non-stop sense of humor I worried I might not survive. You had to acquire a taste for his idea of a joke. It took me forty years.

He and my mother once attended a dinner party where someone at the table made the mistake of complimenting my dad's shirt. My father didn't hesitate. "Don't say no one ever gave you the shirt off his back," he's reported to have said, peeling down to bare chest.

My mother couldn't finish her dessert.

You couldn't take him anywhere. In restaurants, he thought a gentleman helped the waitress clear the table and got his own ice water. He made the front page of the Worcester newspaper, pedaling down Main Street on his bicycle in a blizzard. After my mother moved to Florida, he did his laundry by wearing his clothes into the shower.

When I was small, he added one word to his vocabulary every day by using it three times in a sentence. "Don't flagellate yourself about that," he was likely to say to anyone at any time. His version of *Thirty Days to a Better Vocabulary* took him thirty years. A seventh grade dropout, he refused to even glance at my report cards. "I don't need a teacher to tell me about my child," he'd say. Most of my life, I mistakenly thought he wouldn't look because he didn't care.

He filled his pockets with silver dollars and pressed one into the hand of every street person he ever passed. My mother was fond of reminding him that if he'd held onto those solid silver coins, he'd have retired a rich man. He drank cod liver oil like water, and once he gave my mother-in-law-to-be a half-gallon, along with an impassioned lecture. When they met again twenty-five years later, he picked up right where he left off. This time he talked her into taking a quart home with her.

Life with my father was never dull.

I guess I've finally lived long enough to appreciate that. As a child, it was tough to have a father who fled from intimacy as if his life depended on it, but recently, without my needs burdening our relationship, we've become friends.

I was in Florida last week, settling my mother-in-law's estate, when I realized I could call my dad and he couldn't say, "This is costing you a fortune," before hanging up in the middle of my sentence.

I curled up in a chair ready for a long talk.

"I was in the bank," he began, "cashing my social security check for fifteen hundred dollars, and I got impatient with the teller who wanted to count the money twice. 'Look,' I said like a big shot, 'Don't bother to count it again. Believe me, if it's one hundred dollars short, I won't hold you responsible.'

"Would you believe?" He laughed at the sheer chutzpah of the man. "That son-of-a-gun peeled off the top hundred dollar bill with a big flourish and looked me straight in the eye. So I thought, 'Oh-oh, Bill, he's called your bluff this time,' and I took the fourteen hundred as if it were the most natural thing in the world, as if it didn't faze me one bit, and I walked straight out the door without a backward glance."

"You did?" I said, enthralled. He did.

I have Homer for a dad, a man who can turn a trip to the bank into a spell-binding adventure. All his life, the roles of husband and father fit him like shrunken shoes, pinching his toes and cutting off his circulation. The fact that I couldn't shape him to my needs caused me all kinds of pain, but all that is behind us now. Today, barefoot at last, he's magnificent. His vitality holds out the promise that I might be that alive, that fiercely myself, when I reach his age.

You have a right to ask me why I'm telling you this.

I'm not.

I'm telling him.

THE PHONE LINES crackled as my sister, Susan, my brother, Ken, and I tried to make sense of the messages coming from Florida. My dad, eighty-eight, had visited the emergency ward three times in the past few weeks, but the doctors kept sending him home. Dad's niece, Ann, seventy-nine, had tried to advocate for him, but no one had listened to her either. My sister couldn't get a straight story from my dad. My sister-in-law, Barbara, who is a physician, couldn't get his doctor to return her calls.

Two days later Susan declared an emergency. Dad wasn't eating (he'd lost twenty pounds), was urinating blood through a catheter, and was alone in his condo, waiting for the results of some test. In my mind I saw an old man, stoically waiting for death in an air-conditioned apartment, and I thought of the Eskimos, who took their old folks out onto an ice floe and left them there to die.

We do it differently in this culture. The old folks take themselves to the ice floe, its true nature hidden by palm trees and hibiscus blossoms, leaving their children behind. They huddle together, caring for one another. When my mother died four years ago, however, the nature of the place became clearly visible. My dad, alone, felt the cold at last.

Since I had the most flexible schedule, I offered to fly down. The problem was I'd been in bed two days with a back spasm and was just beginning to feel some relief. I could barely straighten up, even with an orthomold binder strapped around my waist.

Nonetheless, I decided to go. I'd have to do the best I could.

On the way to the plane, I visited a physical therapist for a session of electrical stimulation, hoping the muscle would be too tired to cramp. Luckily, the plane was half empty, and I stretched out across three seats. By the time I rented a car and drove to my dad's apartment, he was asleep.

For the first time since my mother died, I slept in her bed.

The next morning, I woke to hear Dad moving around. The night's catch of urine was a deep wine red. I helped him take one pill on an empty stomach, then an hour later, made him eat six tablespoons of oatmeal so he could take a different pill on a full stomach. Ironically, the drug directions came on computer sheets so pale I needed Dad's magnifying glass to read them.

"These are kills, not pills," he said. His stomach was upset, but his sense of humor was intact. Dad drank three glasses of water.

No liquid came through the catheter.

I called his Health Maintenance Organization three times. Dad's doctor's nurse wouldn't come to the phone or return my calls. At noon, I drove to the office. She was behind a desk, scowling.

"This must be awful for you," I began. "I bet you're besieged by demanding people all day long." Her face relaxed. I told her how worried I was. She confided that the test results, which she wouldn't show me, indicated Dad should be hospitalized. However, she needed authorization from the urologist, who'd be out of surgery soon. I returned to find Dad huddled in bed, his catheter bag still empty. He complained of cold feet, so I massaged them for while and wrapped him in a heavy blanket.

"All my life," my dad whispered, as if the words were costing him, "I always said I never got a single benefit from having children, but now I don't know, I may have to take it back." His hands were icy. I wrapped him in an electric blanket and turned on the heat. It was an hour before Dad spoke again. "Linda, see if you can get them to send an ambulance." This was the first time in his life my dad had admitted his need for anything.

Now I was really worried.

I called the HMO again. It was two in the afternoon. I asked to speak to the supervisor. "My dad hasn't urinated all day," I said. "His hands and feet are cold, and he's not moving. I think he's slipping into unconsciousness. We can't wait much longer. Isn't there anything you can do?" She promised to station someone outside the operating room.

While Dad lay motionless in the other room, I called my sister for the fourth time since I'd arrived. Luckily, Dad and I weren't facing an unresponsive HMO alone. Susan had already checked in with my husband, my brother and his wife, and had their suggestions ready for me. We strategized what to do next. Without all their support, I'd have been in a panic, but Susan's voice steadied me, centered me again, assured me I was doing the best I could. I hung up and lay down beside my Dad.

Side by side, we waited.

WHEN THE PHONE finally rang, I was half asleep. A voice assured me that my dad had

finally been placed on "red alert," and that once he reached the hospital, he'd be given immediate emergency attention.

I roused my father. While he put on a shirt and pulled his pants over his catheter and leg bag, I went looking for help. In the parking lot an elderly man named George agreed to help me get the patient from the elevator to my car, but by the time we returned to the apartment to get him, my dad had his second wind.

"I don't need help," he said gruffly, brushing past us. Rather than take the elevator, he jogged down three flights of stairs with the two of us in hot pursuit. George, limping from an operation, kept apologizing to me for not being able to keep up with my dad, who had miraculously revived. For the next twenty-five minutes, my father had enough energy to be a very assertive passenger-seat driver.

This was the dad I was used to: the physical fitness nut, the show-off, the independent cuss who insisted he'd never benefited for one minute from fatherhood. This was the stubborn mule whose philosophy of life could be summed up in one of his favorite stories: As a young man, drowning in New York City's East River, he refused to grab the lifeline a bystander threw to him. "I'm fine. I don't need any help," he says he yelled. When he was swept under a boat for the third time, someone jumped in and pulled him out, still protesting.

This was the man who now had me worried. After all, I'd told more than one HMO official that my father was almost comatose.

"Listen, Dad," I said. "I told them you were very ill. Don't make a liar of me. I want you to enter the hospital in a wheelchair.

73

You're supposed to be at death's door, do you hear me? You have to act sick."

Luckily, there was a wheelchair at the hospital entrance. I leaped out of the car, opened my dad's door, and wrestled him into it. An orderly pushed my father toward the entrance while I parked. Then I went to Admissions where my dad, the showman who can't resist an audience, was energetically holding court.

A marine would have envied his posture, even in a wheelchair. He was speaking loudly, gesturing grandly, handing out compliments, making jokes, regaling the admissions lady with the details of his illness. When she left to run his card through a machine, I crouched down beside him.

"Stop it," I hissed. "Remember you're sick!"

"But it was hopeless," I told my sister, when I called from a pay phone the minute he was taken upstairs. "I was waiting for a letter to give to the airlines so that I wouldn't have to pay full fare, and I heard the admissions officer saying, 'His daughter said what? Well, I saw no evidence of that!' Then she gave me a look you wouldn't believe. I felt like strangling Dad with his own catheter."

"You should have thrown him to the floor and said, 'You want sick, I'll give you sick,'" Susan said, and in our shared laughter, I felt myself relax. Dad might turn his illness into an obstacle course but, bathed in glory or not, I'd gotten past the first hurdle. Now I had to make sure Dad's doctors kept us informed.

I saw my dad a few hours later. He'd been dozing.

"Boy, did I need that sleep," he said, "You need strength to die." By then the doctors had pinpointed failing kidneys and blocked ureters, though, as it turned out, they had totally missed the disease causing his problems. Diagnostic procedures would keep my dad hospitalized until my brother and his family arrived to take my place.

"Dad," I said. "When the time comes, I'm expecting you to climb out of your coffin and throw yourself into your own grave."

My dad smiled. Then the pain returned. "I'm fine now, Linda. You can go."

I didn't go, of course. I sat by his bed on and off for the next two days. The nurses may have thought they had a failing old man in their charge, but they were blind to his true nature. In this hospital bed was an eternal vaudevillian, on stage until the very last moment, still working on his latest song-and-dance routine.

That's how I see him now, unabashed and unbeaten, his eyes sparkling under bushy gray eyebrows, his mouth curved into a young boy's mischievous grin. Not as long as he lives, but as long as I live, my dad will be giving the best performance of his life to the folks in the orchestra.

March 1994

I HANG HERE SUSPENDED between birth and death.

My older daughter, Laura, is having early contractions. My father's great-grandchild is making its presence unmistakably felt even as his children sit by his bed, waiting for him to die.

Three weeks ago, after my father was discharged from the hospital, my brother, Ken, his wife, Barbara, and their children went to Florida to bring my dad back to his condo in hopes that he could return to a fully independent life. The news was bleak. The doctors said his earlier prostate cancer had not recurred, but his ureters, which had been blasted by radiation treatments, no longer worked. We were told he'd have to live with tubes exiting from both kidneys for the rest of his life.

It was hard to imagine my father as an invalid. This was a man who only months ago had been winning tennis matches, whose good health was essential to his sense of himself. Ken and Barbara, convinced that the care my dad was getting from his HMO was sub-standard, brought him to the University of Miami to see one of the top urologists in the country, and there we found out how truly inadequate his HMO had been. At last he was correctly diagnosed with an incurable, fast-growing prostate cancer. Now a life of invalidism was replaced with no life at all, and my father knew it.

He discontinued his antibiotics, though his open kidneys

were an invitation to infection. He refused chemotherapy. He stopped eating solids. And my sister, Susan, and her husband, Pierce, the last of us to fly south, went to Boca Raton to bring my father home to die.

I met them at Logan Airport in Boston with a wheelchair and a rented van, and we transported my dad to their home in Waltham. Within twenty-four hours, Hospice West had set up a plan that set my father's heart completely at ease. At his request, they promised him sufficient medication so that he need never spend another sleepless night nor feel the pain he rated a "10" for the Hospice nurse. Susan and Pierce were also reassured by Hospice's careful attention to their needs: the daily visits of a nurse and a home health aide, a round-the-clock nursing care hotline, and unrushed, compassionate, ongoing support.

Now all that was left of my dad's journey was for us to accompany him to the point of his departure.

We were astounded when my dad, who was wrapped in quilts on the couch next to Susan and Pierce's blazing woodstove, whispered, "This is wonderful."

"Dad's having a hard death, but he's having a good death," Susan said. "He has no choice but to accept being loved and cared for in a way he never could before."

If there is a meaning to suffering, this must be it: In its shadow, we are sometimes given a last chance to see one another anew. The reality of his own death has stripped my dad of the personality traits that once kept him distant from the people who loved him. In its place, we meet a new man, freed of the defenses he's always used to guard himself from hurt. The father whose words and actions helped define the adults we are today has vanished. We see the boy he was before the damage was done, a vessel into which it is possible to pour our love.

Dad's openness has caught us all — including him — by surprise. In accepting our help, in his newfound ability to express gratitude, he has given us, his children, the opportunity to be better than we are, to settle our differences without anger, to minister to him, to contribute each in our own way, without recrimination. He has allowed us to see ourselves at last as a loving family.

"My mother never said she loved me," Dad reminisces one afternoon as the dusk gathers outside.

"Yes, I know," I say.

"When she was dying, I was sitting beside her bed. I put my hand on her forehead." He pauses, remembering. This is a story I've never heard before. "After a while, I took it away. I thought she was sleeping. Then, she took my hand and placed it back on her forehead." He chuckles. "She must have taken some comfort from me. I've always thought that was it, the sign."

"The sign of what?" I ask, though I think I know the answer.

"Well, her way of letting me know that I was a good son."

"It was her last gift to you, Dad. Just as this time together is your last gift to your children," I add, gently stroking the hand he has slipped into mine.

Someday I will tell this story to his great-grandchild, who is impatiently waiting in the wings.

Sister

FAMILY PUZZLES

March 1991

THIS WEEK WE CELEBRATED Passover, and it reminded me of those times long ago when our whole family gathered at my grandparents' home — with one significant difference. Unlike the last generation, everyone in my extended family is intermarried except for Jack and me. As a result, I was looking forward to using a new version of the Haggadah, or Passover service, that I'd worked on with my friend Lynn this winter for families with both Jewish and Christian members.

Since Passover is a home-based holiday, we felt free to tinker with the ritual. Fiddling with this particular celebration, trying to make it accessible to children and relevant to life, has always been an important part of keeping Jewish ritual alive. Not only are new theme-based Haggadahs created every year, but in my case, my grandfather, or Zadie, as we called him, had modified the Passover service himself. He'd added a few master touches to enliven the event for his twelve grandchildren.

For example, at one point in the service a glass of wine is placed on the table for the prophet Elijah, and toward the end of the service, the door to the house is opened as a sign that Elijah, the spirit of freedom, is welcome. In most families this is a symbolic act, but Zadie thought we needed something a little more substantial. So he instructed his son, my Uncle Allan, to slip away unnoticed, circle the house, and at the proper moment, come in the front door covered with a white sheet. We grandchildren divided into two camps: the "babies" who could still be bamboozled, and the older kids who'd noticed that Elijah was wearing Allan's shoes. When Allan returned to the table, he always swore he'd been in the bathroom.

Hiding the matzoh, the flat "bread of affliction" that Moses and the Jewish people carried into the desert with them as they hurried to escape from their slavery in Egypt, was another tradition that met with Zadie's special touch. While most families hide a special broken piece of matzoh in another part of the house in order to lure restless children away from the table, Zadie kept his stash between two pillows on the chair next to him. During the meal, I and my cousins would crawl over feet under the huge makeshift dining room table, hoping to grab a piece, our hearts beating at the thought that Zadie might grab a hand, as he did every so often, and demand, "Who's this? Oh, no, you don't. Go back to your seat."

Zadie had a stern voice and a keen eye. His grandchildren never ceased to be amazed at how easy it was to outwit him.

Now that my mother is gone and my dad is in Florida, I'm the oldest child and head of our family by default. There have been two generations at our Passover table for a long while, but this time our extended family included Jessie, my brand-new granddaughter, Sam, my brother's three-year old son, and Sarah, his infant daughter. It felt quite different to be the oldest of three generations. I felt the tug of the past. I wanted my nephew to have the same experience I'd had.

"Shall I ask someone to play Elijah?" I asked my brother, Ken.

"My God, no!" he shot back. "Sam's already terrified of Ninja turtles and dinosaurs. He'll take one look at Elijah and have nightmares for a month."

We agreed to postpone Elijah's appearance for another year. With my husband in Florida visiting his mother, I appointed Ken to guard the matzoh.

The service went splendidly, but speedily. Hunger has this amazing ability to make people plow through the text like Pac-Men, gobbling up one word after another. We raced along at a slick pace until it was time to break and hide the matzoh.

"Now I'm going to keep an eye on this," Ken said, stuffing several pieces of matzoh between pillows on the empty chair next to him. "Nobody take any." He paused for effect. "But, Sam, if you happen to get some, you get a prize when you return it to me."

Sam heard the first part, the "nobody-take-any" part, so when his mother encouraged him to get the matzoh, he solemnly informed her that his dad had told him not to. When his Aunt Susan urged him to climb under the table, he frowned and told her his dad would get mad.

"Sam, you're supposed to go find it," I said.

"Dad, I'm gonna come get the matzoh," he announced.

His father imitated Zadie perfectly. "I didn't hear anything," he said. Sam wouldn't budge. It was an impasse. In desperation I took Sam's hand and pulled him under the table with me. We crawled toward the chair with the pillows. All Sam had to do was reach out and the prize was his. Instead he tugged on his dad's pant leg.

"Hey, Dad," he said, "I'm taking the matzoh. Okay?"

How can I explain what a joy it was to see the world with the eyes of a child? I saw how big my brother was and felt the weight of his authority. Our table grew as huge as my grandparents' had been years ago, the quest for the matzoh every bit as great an adventure. Somehow, when my children were small, I'd been so busy running things that I hadn't seen that this ritual was a way of passing along our past to another generation.

"I can't believe I'm sitting in Zadie's place," Ken said to me. I felt the same amazement at finding myself in a role I had once viewed with respect and something akin to awe. Our parents never had a seder. My brother, my sister, and I had to skip the generation above and add a generation below before our history broke through and caught us up in its wondrous power.

July 1993

MY BROTHER AND HIS family spent the Fourth of July weekend with us. Each morning Ken tucked his two-and-a-half-year-old daughter into our bed before going back to sleep himself. Sarah, snuggled between Jack and me, wanted companionship, so we entertained her by singing a song she absolutely adored. It went:

There were ten in the bed when Sarah said,
'Roll over. Roll over.'
So they all rolled over and Jack fell out.
There were nine in the bed when . . .

We sang until everyone in our family had fallen out of bed, there was only one left, and the little one says sadly, "I'm lonely."

82

"That's odd," said my brother, coming in to collect Sarah for breakfast, "I thought the last one said, 'Good night!' " He pronounced the last two words with great cheerfulness.

Weeks later, that tune is still running in my head, but so are the two different endings, which seem to express the conflict raging at the heart of this culture. This is the question: When you've cleared the deck of all the people getting in your way, will you be happy or lonely?

This culture enthusiastically promotes the latter position. It says: Other people are a pain in the neck, constantly impinging upon your freedom to do whatever you want to do. They clog up the highways, get in front of you in line, and push you around when they get the chance. As a result, women who wish to make something of their lives are encouraged to avoid early entanglements because of the fear that men will drain them dry with their demands. Men, on the other hand, shy away from commitment because it is widely believed that the responsibilities of marriage will suck the life out of them.

From this perspective, singles are the lucky ones, free to travel, spend their money as they choose, find exciting new partners at will, and even pick a movie without first having to engage in lengthy consultation. When these independent folks have rolled the others out of bed, they grab the pillows, hog the covers, and stretch out for a luxurious night's sleep, knowing they can watch TV, eat in bed, or read, without ever having to take anyone else into consideration.

Is this not happiness? Ah, but here's the rub.

It is, but only if we see the world as a place where we're all in competition — for a limited amount of money, for control, for the most comfortable spot on the mattress. Then other folks are adversaries, no matter how much they love us. But if you're a person who values sharing more than purchasing, or who's intrigued by the idea of being enlarged by someone else's interests, it's a different story. For some of us, the deprivations of sharing a bed — in my case, having a dog who lies on my feet and a husband who's banished TV from our bedroom and can't sleep with my reading light on — are more than made up for by the pleasures of his company, from late-night conversations, to reading aloud from our current book, to snuggling.

Sarah's song was actually a metaphor for this Fourth of July when there were eight in the beds, including Jack and me. Ken and Barbara filled one room, their children another, and my daughter, Julie and her husband, Chris, occupied her old bedroom. My granddaughter napped wherever she fell. Since we'd planned a Fourth of July party with fifty guests, the laundry piled up, toys migrated, food vanished, the dishwasher filled, the noise level soared, and — guess what — I enjoyed the chaos.

As I grow older, I'm more aware that my attempts to control my environment actually deaden reality, shaping a wild flow of activity into something familiar, predictable, and sterile. I'm convinced that when I try to have everything just the way I prefer it, I end up destroying spontaneity. I'm blinded to the joy of responding to the world's diversions. I set myself at odds with the life swirling around me.

Alone, I peer at the world through the filter of my own beliefs. In the company of others, I'm challenged by opinions that challenge my own. Alone, I'm limited by my preferences, my inhibitions, my narcissism. In association, I can be carried away by others' enthusiasm, motivated by their tolerance, enlivened by their presence. Looking at my life, I have come to see that without help, I could never have escaped the constriction of my limited expectations.

Should Jack and I be encouraging Sarah to claim the bed all for herself with a cheerful "Good night?" Afraid not. By the time the three of us had musically heaved the dog out of our bed for the umpteenth time, we were all convinced that a bed crowded with sleepyheads was a stopover in heaven.

October 1993

I WOKE UP SUNDAY in a terrible mood. My husband and I had visited my brother and his family the day before, and in retrospect, I was angry at something my brother had failed to say. I wore a scowl to breakfast.

"Linda," said my husband, "aren't you an advocate for not burying grievances? Don't walk around grumbling to yourself that Ken's ungrateful. Call him and have this out with him."

"Why bother?" I asked. "He's visiting his in-laws for Thanksgiving, and by Christmas I'll have forgotten it. Now I'm glad he's not coming here for Thanksgiving."

"I don't believe this. You know you'll feel better . . . "

The phone rang. I was relieved at the interruption. I wasn't ready to call Ken yet. I had to cool down. I had to plan what I wanted to say.

I picked up the phone.

Just my luck, it was my brother.

I'm confessing to my own reluctance to say what I felt just to make clear that I know how difficult my own advice is to follow. Face it, we're all cowards when it comes to confronting someone important to us. Nursing an injury keeps it under your control; discussing it is dangerous. Words can blow up in your face. Who wants to begin a process when you can't predict the outcome? Who doesn't wish for an easier way out?

But there was my husband, sending me meaningful looks. And there was my brother on the phone, presenting me with the opportunity to tell him that I felt unappreciated. I probably wouldn't have bothered saying anything if we weren't from the same family, if his faults weren't mine as well, but we both have the same problem expressing gratitude, and I'm finally learning how much difference it can make to acknowledge a good turn. I thought my insights might be of some help to him.

I had to grow up before I became aware that I rarely acknowledged the nice things people did for me. I learned it the hard way, by having my family point out to me how often I neither noticed nor said thank you for favors. I wasn't always pleased to have this pointed out, however, and since we come from the same background, I suspected Ken wouldn't be either.

After all, we'd had the same upbringing.

Most of us are taught as children to say "Thank you" whether we feel like it or not, with the result that expressing appreciation becomes good manners rather than a sincere expression of feeling, but in my family, we weren't even taught that. My dad seemed to feel that recognizing a debt created an obligation to do something bigger in return, and that ignoring someone else's good deed erased it. I think he felt as if acknowledging a favor diminished both his independence and his pride in himself. In fact, I think my dad was so committed to seeing himself as needing no one's help that being grateful would have required a change in his self-image. Feeling grateful came to seem so shameful that the first thank-you notes I ever wrote were for wedding presents, and I sent them only because all the wedding books said it was necessary.

It wasn't until I attended the Option Institute that I caught a glimpse of the fact that appreciation also benefits the one expressing it.

"We don't cheat the world with our lack of gratitude; we cheat only ourselves," Barry Neil Kaufman once said in class, citing thankfulness as one of six powerful and effective shortcuts to happiness. It is only as an adult that I've come to understand that when we count our blessings instead of overlooking them, personal problems seem less overwhelming. When we carefully note the instances of generosity shown us by family and friends, we feel luckier, more lighthearted, more hopeful, *and* more loved.

I wanted to tell my brother he'd be happier if he paid more attention to the kindnesses shown him.

In this particular case, by me.

It was hard to jump right in and tell Ken I felt hurt, but I did. To wipe the slate absolutely clean, I threw in a few other recent examples of nice things I'd done that he hadn't acknowledged.

Since I felt guilty for needing positive feedback, I didn't do such a good job of it. Since Ken was taken by surprise, neither did he.

Still, after he'd had a few hours to assimilate our conversation, he called me back, and we both explained ourselves all over again. A few days later, Ken's son, Sam, called to thank me for his birthday gift. Then Ken got on the phone. The jangling space between us was gone.

ster

Each time this happens, I'm surprised that I can reveal my true feelings and still be loved; that I can be myself and still be accepted; that I can take the emotions that distance me, and by sharing them, regain the closeness I want so much. Each time this happens, I rediscover that the people in my life care about me.

I may have been out of line when I spoke to my brother, but because it mattered to me, it mattered to him. All the more reason to tell him one more time how much I appreciate him.

April 1994*

MY FATHER DIED peacefully in his sleep by the woodstove in Susan's living room. Our family decided to hold a memorial service for him at Bigelow Chapel, a tiny Gothic rose-windowed gem at the Mount Auburn cemetery. In the process of creating an order of service, hiring an organist, and covering a bulletin board with photos, we discovered, to no one's surprise, that all three children and each of their mates wanted to deliver a eulogy.

We all seem to have inherited my dad's love of a good story and his conviction that no one else could do it justice.

My father was, as I recalled when it was my turn to speak, more himself than any person I have ever known. As we remembered him that day — in my sister-in-law's poem, in my brother-in-law's short story, in my fiction — the behavior that had once embarrassed us now elicited feelings of admiration. My brother made everyone laugh, recalling the unorthodox maxims my dad had passed on to him. My husband read a poem about why he now passes out silver dollars to strangers, a practice my dad followed all his life. We paid tribute to an unrelenting, unashamed, nonconformist by refusing to bury my father's outrageousness along with his body.

My sister took another tack, speaking of her struggle to live through the changes of her life with grace and compassion. In a room filled with the fragrance of lilies, in the shimmering light of stained glass windows, Susan began:

"My father had a huge notice in block letters on his refrigerator that read: 'In the event of my death, call the Florida Cremation Society.' I'm sure my father got pleasure and amusement from the reaction to that notice from those intrepid enough to visit him.

"I have a poem on my refrigerator by a thirteenth century Sufi mystical poet, Rumi. It begins: *You are bitter because you were not up to the magnitude of the pain that was entrusted to you.*

"That is how I've felt since my father's death — not bitter, but unequal to the measure of suffering. I dream my father back alive at night, or hear in the late afternoon one of my father's soft moans I recently became so attuned to.

"Rumi goes on: *Meet it in gladness instead of self-pity. Offer your heart as a vehicle to transform the world's suffering into joy.*

"I have not yet fathomed how to transform suffering into joy, though I suspect it has something to do with that note on my dad's refrigerator. Astoundingly, my father met his death with the same vigor, will, and fascinated, determined engagement with which he met everything else in life that interested him. He didn't shrink from the enormity of the mystery. He took no refuge in self-pity, anger, shame, or doubt. He was not bitter upon receiving his endowment. He was equal to its magnitude.

"I could only watch — and attend — as the living body became a corpse, and when it was over, I could not take it in. So, for me, death remains a mystery, a locked book whose clasp I cannot even touch. Perhaps someday I will be able — if not to transform the world's suffering into joy — at least to claim, as my father did, as he clasped a cherry Popsicle I gave him after he was no longer able to drink from his cup, that I am shaking hands with God."

Listening to the members of my extended family speak, I marveled at the way caring for our last parent as he died had summoned forth our best selves. Somehow during this time of grief, we not only relied upon each other's strengths, but were willing to make up for each other's weaknesses without blame or reproach.

I had been relieved by how well we were getting along until, a week before his death, my father came up with the idea of changing his will. Whether my dad was uncomfortable with our unusual family harmony, or was motivated by the wish to make amends to my brother in the only way still open to him, he set off a fire storm of emotions by stating his intention to shift the settlement between Susan and Ken in my brother's favor. After a tense afternoon, we all gathered in the den while my dad lay on the living room couch, unaware of the maelstrom of suspicion, resentment, and hurt he'd set in motion.

We were all shaken, worried that the cooperation we'd so far managed to maintain would break down and leave us at odds forever. With feelings running high, it seemed impossible to settle the matter to everyone's satisfaction until Susan suggested that we postpone dealing with the specifics of Dad's last wishes until after his death.

"Let's trust each other and trust that, when the time comes, we'll deal with each other fairly," she said.

We all nodded, grateful that she'd come up with a way to avoid an explosive confrontation. So, it seems, was my dad, who didn't mention the matter again. His will was never changed.

In fact, days before he died, my father expressed only one regret — the fact that he'd miss his own funeral.

There must be some way to make sure he finds out his story has a happy ending, that not only our better selves, but his, prevailed.

God, please forward.

September 1996

YEARS AGO, WHEN women's liberation was in its first flowering, my younger sister, Susan, wrote a short story about a woman who was learning to repair her car engine. I thought it was one of the best depictions I'd ever seen of the self-doubt that troubled women as they attempted to master activities previously reserved for men. I was a young mother at the time, but I identified with the heroine and thought the story perfectly captured the preoccupations of a generation about to plunge into an era of momentous change.

Susan never even tried to get the story published.

Fast forward twenty-five years. My sister's written a novel. Actually, it might be more accurate to say she's been writing and rewriting a novel for the last fifteen years, trying to avoid that end point that has tripped her up time and again — the moment of reckoning when you submit the best you can do to another's judgment and find out whether your dreams have been the pathway to a new life or a hopeless illusion.

This time my sister did take that difficult, but crucial, final step. She sent her manuscript out to various agents. But don't look for the name Susan Holbert on the best-seller list yet. So far, a dozen "experts" on literary merit have sent the manuscript back. Susan is finally face-to-face with the monster who has intimidated her all her life — a creature called rejection.

"I think I had this vision," she told me, "that one day my novel would be published, and all those people who thought I was ordinary and unremarkable would have to revise their opinions of me and see what a talented person I really was. Writing a successful and acclaimed novel was the act that was going to reveal my true nature to everyone, but putting that burden on my writing made the stakes so high that it almost paralyzed me.

"Now I see it differently," she continued. "The real task of my life is just what my book is about: to learn to deal with rejection and not be devastated by it. Every time the manuscript comes back and I don't die, I get stronger. I need to learn, deep inside where it counts, that I'm not somebody else's opinion of me, that I can value myself without having to have some extraordinary accomplishment to my name. I've come to feel that I need to go through this process until it no longer hurts, and then whatever happens with the book will be fine."

I listened to Susan, remembering how she was just recovering from two years of intermittent bed rest when a wave caught her on a rocky bluff in Gloucester and threw her down, bone against stone, exacerbating an already debilitatingly weak back. She does not drive now and can rarely manage the ride from her home in

Waltham to mine in Marblehead. She is to some degree an invalid.

It isn't easy to make a living when you can't ride to work or sit at a desk, but Susan discovered she had a talent for book indexing, a task done by free-lancers who work at home. She rolls the computer next to her bed, and with the keyboard on her knees, has indexed everything from Lotus 1-2-3 to the autobiography of Rosalynn Carter. She could have concentrated solely on her own career, as she moved through trade and textbooks to the fast-paced world of computer software. Instead she began teaching indexing courses, sharing her skills with at-home mothers, caretakers, and folks in wheelchairs. With the help of a organization for the handicapped, Susan prepared a video three years ago for people who could not leave home even to attend her day-long workshops. In the past ten years, she has offered countless people who preferred, or were forced by circumstance, to work at home, the opportunity to make a decent living.

Why isn't this her extraordinary accomplishment? Why are we so dismissive of those parts of our lives that don't bring with them fame, great wealth, or public acclaim? I hear Susan's doubts about her worth echoed everywhere I go. I know I would be feeling them myself if I hadn't attained a certain confirmation of merit through my column.

What's so hard to understand is that feelings of insignificance plague us all, no matter what we've achieved. I once heard movie star Ali McGraw, a college classmate of mine, explain to a television interviewer that she wasn't attending our tenth college reunion because she felt she hadn't yet accomplished anything worthwhile. All I have to do is conjure up the names of Pulitzer Prize winners, or skim the best-seller list, or read *People* magazine to realize that, in the world's reckoning, I haven't amounted to all that much.

There's no relief from this in a culture that extols a very few winners and ignores the rest of us. We must have the courage to proclaim, not only to those we love but to ourselves as well, that the only true measure of worth is how much we contribute to the well-being of those whose lives we touch.

FAMILY PUZZLES

I'VE BEEN THINKING about my sister's unpublished novel.

The heroine's life is similar in many ways to my sister's, and the heroine's parents are the spitting image of my own. But the heroine in *Making Waves* has no siblings, and so I don't have to worry about any role I might play. I'm free to concentrate on the story and, I must admit, I'm shocked to see how similarly Susan and I view our folks.

There are seven years between the two of us, a lifetime really, if you understand that I was born at a time when my parents were living with my father's mother and fighting over my father's attachment to her. I was born on that battlefield, becoming the one my mother could choose over my dad to pay him back for having chosen his mother over her. After my sister was born, my parents moved into one floor of a triple-decker just below my mother's mother, which brought its own set of tensions. Soon after my brother was born five years later, we'd become affluent enough to move into our own home.

My parents had struggled to provide me with a playmate, undergoing all kinds of procedures to have a second child. By the time they succeeded, however, I was used to being an only child and resented having Susan thrust into my life. By the time my brother was born, I was resigned to siblings, and I remember feeling maternal toward the baby of the family. Still, I left for college when Susan was eleven and Ken was six. When I married three years later, Susan, thirteen, was a bridesmaid, and Ken, eight, was the ringbearer.

If my parents still held onto some idea of us becoming friends, it was a long way off in the future.

There were obstacles to surmount before we could meet as equals. For starters, there were all those years between us. Then there was the fact that our parents were in different stages of life when each of us was born, giving us three wildly different childhoods. My husband and I tended to treat Ken as if he were our child, which he resented. When Susan and her boyfriend moved in with us after their commune burned down in the early seventies, there was an almost unbreachable generational gulf between my role as a wife and mother and Susan's embrace of radical feminism.

Whole years passed when one of us wasn't talking to another, when any message we had to deliver went through my mother, even though we were all adults. I recall sitting across a table from Susan in the late seventies, proclaiming, "Look, there's no law that says we have to be friends." At the time I imagined I was setting myself loose from all familial claims, and yet here we three siblings are, two decades later, still working on how three such different individuals can become true friends.

Part of the reason must be that the parents in Susan's novel are as familiar to me as my own face in the mirror.

Her heroine confronts a mother who shrugs, a gesture that is taken to mean "I'm hopeless. So? Go do me something," and I remember the frustration I felt when my mother used almost the same words with me: "That's just the way I am. Take it or leave it!" I hear my mom's voice clear as a bell when this fictional mother says to Susan's heroine, "Never marry a man thinking he'll change." I recognize the infuriating father who disrupts everyone's dinner plans by refusing to say what time he'll be home from work, and the outrageous father whose sole aim in life seems to be finding a place to sunbathe nude. When I read that Susan's fictional father pushes his partner "around the floor like a wheelbarrow," my own dad got up out of my imagination and demonstrated the meringue steps he learned at Arthur Murray's right in my living room.

Readers will surely admire Susan's ability to create such zany folks. "What an imagination," they'll think. "How did she ever come up with such a bizarre cast of characters?"

Who else but siblings could have ever considered these people normal? Who else but flesh-and-blood would be flooded with nostalgia for the old three-ring circus? My sister, my brother, and I are the only people on this planet who have spent a lifetime in thrall to the two adults whose feelings toward each other were an unsolved mystery.

That mystery didn't end with our parents' deaths. Our parents live on in us in the various traits we've taken from them and now embody, for better or worse. I'm continually bumping into my past, not only in Susan's fiction, but embedded in my siblings. They set off ancient alarms, making me think I'm home again. A familiar brusqueness in my brother, a well-known lack of confidence in Susan is like the sprinkle of salt on old wounds.

Perhaps this is why we still struggle, why we continue to hold onto one another so tightly: Until we, too, vanish from the earth, my brother, sister, and I are each other's best and only chance to heal the wounds of the past.

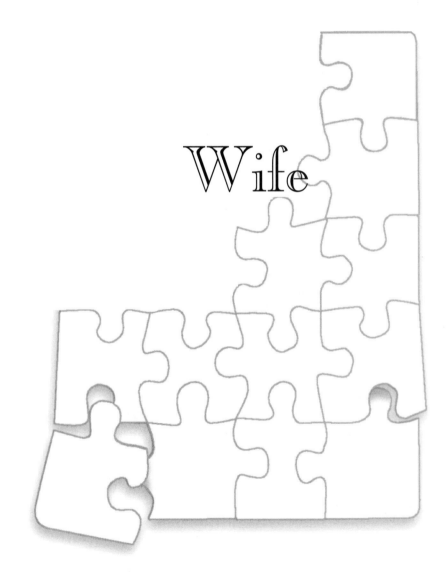

Wife

October 1985

WHEN I WAS FIRST MARRIED, I used to go to my husband's closet on chilly afternoons and find a warm flannel shirt. I'd roll up the sleeves and putter around the house, cozy as could be. Then Jack would come home and hit the roof.

"I wish you'd ask before taking my things," he'd say sternly.

"If you don't want me to wear your clothes, I won't wear them," I'd reply icily, tearing the shirt off my back.

"Hon, I don't mind if you wear them. I just want you to ask first."

"You're not home. How can I ask?" I'd reply. Or, "Why do you care? You never wear it!" Or, "What harm am I doing to your precious shirt?"

I never paid attention to Jack's answers. Why couldn't he see that if I'd merely wanted something warm to wear, I'd have put on my own sweater or bought a flannel shirt? I wanted my husband to understand my need to treat his possessions as if they were mine. Instead, he saw my desire to merge as something to defend himself against.

"Sweetheart," he'd say, trying to calm me, "you don't seem to understand the concept of personal boundaries."

That tone, those words, the implications. I'd immediately become hysterical.

I perceived him as rigid and unfeeling. He cared more about things than he did about me, whose only crime was to love him so much I wanted to wear his stupid shirts. My college roommates had slept in their boyfriends' pajamas. They knew a date's wool scarf was twice as warm as one you'd bought yourself. Why did my husband have to reject me by putting barriers between us? I'd wrap self-pity around me like a suit of armor. I'd rattle it self-righteously at Jack, but after a while I'd recall that he cared a great deal about me and not at all about his possessions, and things would return to normal.

Until the next time.

We stopped fighting about his flannel shirts when I stopped borrowing them, not when I learned to ask.

I never learned to ask.

After all, as a mother, I had no use for possessive pronouns. There was no such thing as "my" kitchen, "my" time, "my" interests. In fact, at one point I couldn't even find "my" chance to go to the bathroom by myself. When I did try to set limits, my wishes were often overruled by my children's crying or fussiness or hunger. I lived in response to two needy beings who weren't due to pick up the concept of asking permission for a while. My husband lived in a realm where an adult's wishes were always taken into account. He observed me with amazement; I viewed him with alarm. Once we stopped taking such behavior personally, we learned to co-exist.

Except now that the children have left, and there are only the two of us here, I'm turning into his former self: I'm becoming as territorial as a Siamese Fighting Fish.

I have my own office and everything in it is in a place where I can find it. I have my kitchen back, and no one messes up the cabinets but me. I have a closet from which my clothes no longer disappear and a pocketbook from which no one takes my car keys. I have a chalkboard with only my scribbles on it, a car littered with my own trash, a library card that reflects only my own overdue books.

I also have a calendar on which I keep all the important dates of my life and a computer I bought with money I earned myself. I never dreamed that one day I'd be this rigid and unfeeling, but here goes: I wish my husband would keep his hands off them.

Take the calendar. I want Jack to record his visit to his mother, but must he fill the Friday box with "FL," all of Saturday with "OR," all of Sunday with "IDA"? Must he write "Mtg at Stan O's" in felt-tip pen on Tuesday, cross it out and scribble it in pen the following Thursday? He's forcing me into the margins with his abbreviations, his scrawling handwriting, his duplications.

And then there is my computer. In the evening he's been using it at my desk, blocking access to my files, and answering his calls on my phone. Sometimes he puts my disks in the wrong place, leaves his notes among my papers, and forgets to replace the dust cover on my Mac.

I wish he'd ask if he could use them.

I like saying, "No."

M Y   H U S B A N D, a psychiatrist, was invited to give a speech in Atlanta. We flew down a day early to squeeze in a romantic mini-vacation. We arrived late and fell into bed. In the morning I was in the mood for love.

"I feel depressed." Those were my husband's first words. Then he went into the bathroom. He reappeared, brushing his teeth. "My dad died a year ago today," he said.

"Well, that's that," I remember thinking, trying to stop feeling anything. After all, you can't get mad because someone's in grief. Good wives are good sports, willing to put aside their own wishes when something more important comes along. I put on a resigned smile and went out to breakfast with him.

We both should have stayed in bed.

In one day we got into an automobile accident, spent two hours with the police, had my husband's license taken into police possession, were assigned a court date we couldn't make, and acquired a lawyer. We missed lunch and found that the play we'd planned on seeing that night was sold out. Turning out the light before I went to bed, I got a painful electric shock from the bedside lamp. The trip was so awful we couldn't discuss it for weeks.

"We were definitely an accident waiting to happen," I said to my husband later, "but what could we have done differently?"

"I wish you'd asked me how I felt that morning," he said.

I know Jack's right. If I'd asked about his feelings, he could have explored them, and I would have had a chance to express mine. We could have compromised, say, allowing him some time for grieving, or gone our separate ways for part of the day. Perhaps, feeling understood, my husband could have put his sadness aside for some other time.

I didn't ask any questions. In fact, I made it clear I didn't want to talk because I'd made up answers to my satisfaction. I'd already decided Jack didn't care how disappointed I was. I judged him emotionally self-indulgent. I saw myself playing saint to a cad. Still, would I have chosen playing that role over having a good time? Not if I'd known then what I know now, that many of our difficulties can be solved by what Barry Neil Kaufman, in his book *Happiness Is a Choice*, calls "the gift of a question."

Not any question will do, of course.

Questions such as, "Why do you always ruin things?" are really negative judgments. So are questions that express personal distress, such as, "How could you have done that to me?" Or questions that allow for only one answer, such as, "You're not going to do that again, are you?" Questions can disguise demands, express scorn, often do everything but illuminate the situation.

It's no wonder we so often resent them.

Still, there are questions that allow people to explore their feelings and beliefs, that provide a chance to examine relationships or discover hidden motives. These questions spring from true concern and have no goal except to allow one person to reveal herself to another. They're scary questions, such as, "What do you mean?" or "Why did you do that?" or "What do you want?" or "How do you feel?" If asked with openness and genuine interest, they make the path ahead suddenly unpredictable and full of promise.

It takes courage to seek the truth. We need to have psychic space for the new information that appears when we avoid jumping to conclusions. We also have to be willing to be changed, to accommodate and grow.

I'm reminded of a friend who almost came to blows with her grown son over her way of waking him up for work. "Have you ever asked him how he wants you to wake him," someone asked her, "or how he thinks you can help?" Even she was surprised those questions had never occurred to her.

The problem is we love people whom we don't understand, and instead of being optimistic and curious, we invent reasons for their behavior that usually make us angry. When they respond by counterattacking or becoming defensive, we deprive them of the chance to understand themselves as well.

How often do we investigate what's really happening before adopting an attitude? And how often do we really accept the answers to our questions? If you're anything like me, not nearly often enough.

The cliché insists love is the answer.

Perhaps love is the question.

April 1988

WHEN MY HUSBAND came back from Zambia last August, I was enrolled in a month-long personal growth program at the Option Institute. Jack came for the weekend. I was waiting in the lobby of a nearby inn as he arrived, but when I went to hug him, he backed away.

"This is the good news," Jack said. "I fell off my bike and cracked two ribs. You'll have to hug me gently for a while."

"If that's the good news, I'd hate to hear the bad," I joked.

"This is the bad news," he said quietly. "I may have picked up AIDS in Africa."

This is how it happened: As a psychiatrist, my husband hadn't practiced medicine in thirty years, but he had taken a medical textbook and his black bag in case his skills were needed during his week building houses with Habitat for Humanity. When he discovered he was the only doctor within ninety miles of the nearest city, he taught First Aid and ran a clinic in the evenings.

One night a man named Amos came to his clinic with an abscessed leg and a fever of 103. Jack thought the man would die unless the leg was lanced. With only two months of a 1960 surgical rotation under his belt, Jack was still the most competent person to perform the operation. And the most nervous. When he cut into the leg, blood spattered onto his hands, roughened from working with cinder blocks. My husband didn't think Amos' blood had gotten into a cut on his finger covered with a bandage, but he wasn't absolutely certain.

"Why didn't you wear rubber gloves?" I asked.

"I was so anxious, I wasn't thinking clearly," he said.

I understand how panic blocks the ability to think. In fact, I'd spent a good part of my time at Option looking at how my strong emotions got in the way of finding solutions to my own problems.

"What makes you think Amos had AIDS?" I asked.

"Since there's no AIDS testing to speak of in Zambia, there's no way of knowing. It's unclear how long it takes to develop anti-bodies, but I'll get tested at three and six months. Until then, we'll have to be careful."

All month at Option I'd been working on this question: Is

happiness something you fall into when everything's going well, or is it a state of mind you can choose, regardless of circumstance?

I used to think I deserved to be unhappy if I made a mistake or failed to do my best. That way, I'd try harder the next time. I felt I had to be unhappy if someone I loved suffered or if things didn't go the way I wanted. That way I proved to myself, and to others, how much I cared.

This time I was determined to respond in a new way.

If Jack and I were actually free to choose our state of mind, it seemed clear we should choose to be happy. After all, if he didn't have AIDS, it would be criminal to throw away six months of our lives by filling them with needless fears. If he did have AIDS, it was even more important to enjoy those months together. After all, we had something at this moment that we wouldn't have after the diagnosis was made — hope.

The two of us spent a good part of that first evening trying to put ourselves into a frame of mind that would make such a long wait bearable. We didn't want to bury our feelings in the mutual pretense that everything would be fine, but we didn't want to just react, either. In the end, we decided that the best way to keep our minds from dwelling on the terrifying future was by staying attuned to the present moment.

In the weeks and months that followed, this became my favorite affirmation: *I have everything I need to enjoy my here and now.* I repeated it to myself when I came across the news that AIDS patients were being fired and barred from schools, or abandoned by friends and family; when I saw a doctor on TV, who'd pricked himself with a needle, declare it would be five years before he felt safe again.

Just as frightening thoughts produce fear, affirmations can calm and center. Every time I found myself growing anxious or fearful, I did an internal check. Was Jack well right now? Did we have a roof over our heads, friends, satisfying work? Did I have everything I needed to enjoy my here and now? Well, then, I could choose to be happy at that moment. My future was no more uncertain than everyone else's.

This may sound like hocus-pocus, or perhaps just plain foolishness. I can only say that, since there was nothing I could do about whether my husband had contracted AIDS — no second opinions to seek, no miracle drugs to pursue — I decided to work on the one thing within my control: my attitude. I took my fears and set them aside, knowing they would be there in force if I ever needed them. There would be plenty of time to worry.

My husband's second blood test came back last week.

Negative.

Now I'll cry. With relief.

June 1989

I WAS IN THE MIDDLE of an argument with my husband, and I must have been losing. Why else would I have reproached him for something he'd done in the early years of our marriage?

"I'm not the same person I was then," he said.

I was taken aback. In fact I felt robbed.

After all, wasn't his answer a way of evading responsibility for what he'd done in the past? If Jack could simply decide that our past experience was irrelevant to our present relationship, where did that leave me?

Suddenly I understood why families are often reluctant to acknowledge that their child has become someone other than the adult they expected.

In my family we joked that the girls had gotten all the brains until my brother excelled in graduate school. "I don't believe it," my mother had said when she called to tell me. Her voice was tinged with pride, but her words revealed a more ambiguous reaction. She knew this was great news, but Ken's success not only changed her notions about him, it required her to revise the story of her own life.

I mean, if Jack insists he isn't the same person I married, am I still the moody, insecure young woman who walked up the aisle to meet him in 1959? Has experience added new dimensions to my personality, or has the process been one of subtraction, of my letting go of the harmful beliefs that limited my potential? I've been arguing about this with friends for days.

"You're the same person all your life," one of them insists. "You see an old friend at a reunion twenty years later and nothing's changed. You can pick up right where you left off."

"People carry their past with them as subpersonalities," adds another. "You go on a date at forty and up pops the teen you used to be, with all her old insecurities. We're a collection of selves."

My husband believes the idea of a fixed personality is an illusion. "The problem starts when we think we're the particular point of view that we hold at any given moment," he says. "Then it's easy to feel you have defend that point of view in order to be your self. We're subject to our programming, of course, but we can make the decision to recreate ourselves any time we want."

Actually, Jack and I have seen that happen. After a twenty-year rift, his mother changed her feelings about me so quickly it took me months to catch up. Now that I think of it, that's what makes being alive so thrilling. Unless you squeeze the people you love into boxes and keep them there, they'll surprise you every time.

A few days after my argument with Jack, I left home to spend a week at the Option Institute. I was paired with another person and asked to tell about a difficult situation in my life. I described a wrong Jack had done me. Then we were instructed to tell the story again, this time viewing it through the eyes of God.

I balked at first. How could I know God's perspective? An image came to mind: I was floating down a river on a raft. The trip began in white water, where I felt the battering of rock against rubber, the fear of going under and breaking apart, the pull of the crosscurrents. Then we sailed into calm water, and I found myself in a serene, safe place. How could the same drops of water splash in fury one moment, then smooth into a peaceful pool the next? Was the river bad in one instance and good in another? Did it make sense to get angry with it, to blame it, and then punish it with my resentment? If I were rafting through my life, wouldn't I be proud of having gotten through the hard places and delight in the easy stretches? Why should memories undermine my pleasure in peaceful places? Why not accept each turn in the river for what it was?

Perhaps Jack and I aren't the same folks after all these years. It intrigues me to think of my husband as a stream of flowing water. How strange. I've been sailing this particular craft for thirty years, and it's only just occurred to me that I can throw the excess baggage overboard.

October 1992

I RAN INTO A YOUNG friend the other day. He was as groggy as a bear dragged from his lair in the middle of winter.

"You look exhausted," I said. "Aren't you getting any sleep?"

"At our place it's fight 'til you drop," he replied, with a sheepish grin. "My girlfriend insists we never go to bed angry."

Oh, no! Here come all those memories from my past.

The wrangles at midnight. The procession of emotions from speaking to screaming to crying to sobbing. The scorn I felt when my husband expressed concern about being able to get up for work in the morning. The way my worst charges seemed truer as the night wore on. The way I grew more and more self-righteous as the night wore out. The disdain I felt when my husband suggested that we hold each other and go to sleep. The frustration of going around in circles. The point at which I could no longer remember the cause of our argument. And, finally, the next morning's emotional hangover, with its glaze of amnesia.

What in the world had we been doing all night? Nothing worth remembering. So why did we do it?

I was convinced that if I dropped "it" — whatever it was — I'd have to hold on to my rage so I wouldn't forget my arguments. I assumed that if I let my husband get away with something, he'd feel free to do it again. A pushover, I'd be encouraging him to ignore my feelings. I believed that if there were unfinished business between us for a whole night, it would eventually wreck the marriage. I thought that if my husband would just admit he'd been wrong, I could let it go. I thought if we talked long enough, we could make everything right between us.

I was wrong. About all of the above.

Remember when you were small and your mother said, "You're just cranky; you need a nap"? Remember how you hated that?

Well, she was right.

Tired people are more irritable than rested folks, more cantankerous and irascible. People who are sleep-deprived develop impaired judgment, lose their grip on reality, and exhibit signs of mental and emotional confusion. Knowing that keeping people awake is an effective form of torture, why did I ever think it was a way to keep love alive?

I'd heard "Never go to bed angry" so many times I thought it was the eleventh commandment.

I also thought I had to raise a ruckus to be taken seriously. I believed that if I inflicted enough suffering on Jack, he'd think twice before pulling the same trick again. Instead, like a turtle huddled in his shell for self-protection, Jack blanked out most of what I said, waiting out (what he experienced as) my senseless storm of emotions. My extravagant charges, my exaggerated reactions, and words like "never" and "always," which I thought strengthened my case, only distracted and distanced him from what I was trying to communicate. All my arguments only made Jack more defensive.

We couldn't think clearly when we were tired and upset, making our early morning fights totally predictable. By two in the morning, we couldn't have agreed on how long to boil a three-minute egg. By two-thirty, I usually regretted not having gotten a gun permit. By three, Jack was wondering how to obtain an annulment. Lucky for us, it eventually became obvious even to me that I crossed the line from difficult to impossible about an hour past my bedtime. At the same time, my husband turned into a zombie. As we grew older, we grew less resilient. We found it harder to replace what nights of conflict were taking out of us.

So we stopped, less from wisdom than from weariness.

That's when I realized I could trust the love my husband and I felt for one another not to vanish when one or both of us was angry or disappointed or hurt. I'd clung to desperate measures because I lacked confidence that love could co-exist with more troublesome emotions. Sleeping through the night with some difference of opinion unresolved, I discovered all my feelings still intact and accessible the next day. Rested and reasonable, I found that when I clearly stated my objections and said what I wanted, Jack listened attentively. We actually began to make progress on many of the issues that had made our relationship such a stormy one.

It takes guts to challenge those maxims that promise a happy marriage, but the rhythms of the universe back me up.

Have you ever wondered why things are darkest before dawn?

It's nature's way of suggesting we get a good night's sleep.

February 1993

YOU'D THINK BY NOW I'd be resigned to this marriage.

Guess again. Compassion, sympathy, and understanding are useful words in my domestic vocabulary, but *resignation*? To me, it's got the ache of emptiness about it, the feel of hopelessness. I don't plan to resign from dreaming until it's absolutely necessary.

Still, it isn't easy to look at the mate you married eons ago and feel totally blessed to have that person as your life's companion. I don't know how your marriage works, but here's how mine seems to operate in its third decade. Despite all the conflicts we've resolved, and all the wonderful times, old grudges seem to have burrowed into my brain, along with troubling memories I've carried with me for years. Just when we were happiest, some long ago injury, slight, or disappointment, would pop into my mind, casting a long shadow.

As if they were the cloud of bees over Pooh's honey tree, I'd try to brush them away, but they seemed out of my control. Why, when I felt closest to my husband, would I suddenly remember a time he'd let me down or recall an annoying habit of his? These thoughts had a purpose — they got between me and the love I was feeling in the present. Some part of me was fighting to keep a distance I no longer consciously desired.

I hated it. But what could I do about it?

I got angry with myself. That made no difference. I tried willing those thoughts away. They stuck like Velcro. I could have learned to live with them, I suppose. Jack had no idea what was going on in my head, but I have a very low tolerance for misery once I recognize that I'm creating it myself. In one last attempt to understand what I was doing, I made an appointment with an Option mentor.

The Option Institute trains mentors in how to ask direct, open-ended, non-judgmental questions without offering analysis or suggestions. People with an issue to explore allow the mentor's questions to lead them through the maze of beliefs and experiences that influence their behavior and feelings. The aim is to understand why you feel and act the way you do. After that, you get to make up your own mind about whether to change or not.

I signed up for three hour-long sessions with a woman named Gita.

Then I started along a familiar path.

"Let me tell you the terrible things that have happened since I got married," I began. Needless to say, they were everyone else's fault. I did my best to convince Gita of the depth of my suffering, demonstrating how I'd been hurt and misunderstood from the beginning. By the time I was through, a jury would happily have indicted everyone in my life. When I reviewed my story that night, however, it sounded old, even to my ears. I'd gone over this same ground innumerable times — in analysis, in couples' therapy, with friends, alone in my head — and being "right" always turned out to be the same as being miserable. When I returned for a second session, I decided to take a different tack.

"This time I'd like to take responsibility for everything that's gone wrong," I said. I began with the time I'd ruptured a disc at five in the morning and been told by my young husband not to disturb a doctor that early on a Sunday. Still, Jack hadn't kept me from calling. I'd chosen not to reach for the phone, even though I was in agony. Everything that had happened in my adult life carried my seal of approval, in action, if not in words. I made protests, then refused to stand behind them.

If the first session featured a cast of near criminals, the second starred a women who blamed others when she ignored her own best instincts, a woman who dreamed of being rescued, but refused to save herself. Because Gita didn't judge me, I didn't either. I hadn't known any other way, hadn't realized I had the power to act on my own behalf. Nonetheless, I could see I hadn't been the easiest person to live with.

I went into the third session, humbled, wondering how Jack and I had ever managed to stay together all this time.

"Why didn't Jack leave when his sister committed suicide while we were on our honeymoon? He was in such pain. He could have walked away, made a fresh start, left any guilt he felt behind with me."

"Why do you think he stayed?" Gita asked.

"I think he loved me," I said, then sat in tearful silence.

This third session, miraculously, turned into the story of a man and a woman who've always struggled to do their best, often without confidence, or understanding, or the wisdom to see the patterns they were repeating. These folks made mistakes, which were small potatoes compared to their heroic determination, their audacity, their foolhardy capacity for devotion. With this final version, my bitterness drained away.

There's a name for these kinds of folks, even if by now they're wrinkled, or balding, or lost without their bifocals.

Valentines.

May 1993

MY HUSBAND PLAYS the tuba badly. No, wretchedly. Execrably. With unforgettable in-expertise.

After my husband played "When Irish Eyes are Smiling" at my older daughter's wedding as a way of welcoming our son-in-law's Irish family, his father created an award for Jack that read, in part, "for a spontaneous public performance which demonstrated an originality so stark that it stunned the audience, rendering them incapable of meaningful response."

This did not hurt my husband's feelings. He knows the impact his music has. This is a man for whom practice means playing all the notes, right or wrong, at least twice. His tuba, purchased at a yard sale for one hundred dollars, looks as if it's been run over by a truck. His entire repertory consists of five songs, which run the gamut from "Happy Birthday" to "So Long, It's Been Good to Know You."

Still, the phone rings and people ask him to do a gig at some special event, an occurrence that happens more frequently than I might hope. He doesn't get nervous or decide to polish up his technique a bit. He glows. He basks. He's unabashedly delighted. And delightful.

At his first note, audiences burst into hysterical laughter, and the more earnestly my husband attempts to render a recognizable melody, the harder they laugh until they leap to their feet, choking and cheering. I understand why he's in demand. What has been harder for me to figure out is how my husband is perfectly capable of enjoying his tuba solos without ever aiming at competence.

This is not the way I was brought up. Whether it was swimming, tennis, or ballroom dancing, my mother made sure I began with lessons. The pleasure in doing a thing, I was taught, was in doing it well, and so my whole life has been about mastery, whether I was skiing, sewing, or cooking. I never enjoyed trial and error. I wanted to do things as they *should* be done. I disliked looking awkward or amateurish, and to my way of thinking, mistakes took the pleasure out of things. If I felt I'd end up doing something badly, I politely declined the opportunity to begin.

That seemed a perfectly sensible way to operate until I started dancing for exercise three months ago. At the beginning, I gave myself time to learn the steps, but now I'm no longer a novice. Newcomers are catching on while I'm still struggling. I've come to the reluctant conclusion that these complex patterns of movement may never feel like my second nature.

You know what? I don't care.

I can't believe it myself. I feel like stopping people on the street and informing them, "You don't have to be good at something to love it." I want to tell my daughters, "Forget about having to meet your own high standards before you can have a wonderful time." I've learned that it's possible for me to tune in to how good it feels to move without having to submit my performance to my superego for approval.

Oh, what bliss it is to slip past that little inner overachiever!

I admit I was puzzled when frequent repetition didn't lock the order of moves into my brain, but in reading Robert Gardner's book *Frames of Mind: The Theory of Multiple Intelligences*, I have come to have a new respect for what he calls bodily-kinesthetic intelligence, the ability to use one's body in highly differentiated ways. In general, we respect those who rate high in language, logic, and math, but Gardner contends there are other equally important forms of intelligence having to do with music, movement, spatial ability, and personal and interpersonal skills.

These forms of intelligence are like packages under the tree, wondrous gifts given to our species by a generous creator. By opening only those at which we have been trained to excel, we diminish the ways we can express ourselves in the world. The culture colludes, teaching us reading, writing, and arithmetic at an early age, and leaving us to discover our other talents in a hit-and-miss fashion.

Hit, as in hit over the head.

In high school, I was shamed in Glee Club, instructed to *pretend* to sing at concerts because I couldn't hold a tune. I taught myself a few simple songs on the guitar and played them for my children only as long as I could count on their lack of discrimination. Then I stuck the guitar in the closet.

I was so convinced of my lack of grace that, after I tried out for cheerleading and actually made the squad in high school, I never showed up for a single practice.

But my husband and I are proof that it's possible to sing or dance, to play a musical instrument or a sport, to study a foreign language, or calculus, or any other subject that doesn't come easily. All you have to do is allow yourself to step outside the prison of excellence.

January 1994

"WHY DID YOU MARRY ME?" I asked my husband at dinner.

"I was in love with you."

"I know, but what else did you consider? Did you think about whether I could cook or what kind of mother I'd make?"

"I was in love. I didn't think about anything."

Jack swears that statement is true, but it doesn't describe my state of mind. I loved him — but not blindly.

The first time I gazed into his eyes, I knew I was looking at the father of my children. Long before I met Jack, I thought of the man I'd marry as a gift I was giving my unborn children. I didn't view marriage as purely personal. It was also the crucible of family life, and I wasn't about to inflict upon my children the pain I'd experienced as a child.

Jack and I were married for five years before we had a baby. We began by merging our needs and wishes for the good of the whole, but by the early sixties, feminism had redefined togetherness. I brought our daughter home to a world very different from the one I'd entered as a bride. Then I'd taken the word "helpmate" seriously. Now it was important for me to keep track of my separate identity, to make sure that my needs were being met, too.

As the context of our relationship shifted, Jack and I often identified one another as the enemy. I'd been raised to see self-sacrifice as a central aspect of loving. Now I began to see him as standing in the way of my asserting my rights. Jack had been raised to be protective of women. He felt threatened by my angry struggle for self-determination.

It was a tumultuous time, and not only for us. The shock of feminism took its toll on everyone's marriage. All the brave, self-actualized women seemed to be choosing divorce, rejecting male domination. When accusations cut deep and there seemed no end to bitter arguments, the solution seemed to be to take the kids and leave in hopes of starting over. I felt as trampled upon as any of my friends, but I wasn't entirely convinced there was a better world out there somewhere. Still, though I would never have admitted it to anyone at the time, there were days and weeks, and longer, when both of us stayed in this marriage for the sake of the children.

Staying together "for the children's sake" was an old-fashioned concept, now swept away. Where once a stable, though not necessarily happy, home had been deemed essential for children, now anything seemed better than parents in constant conflict. I believed that, but I didn't act upon it. How could I, when I could see every day how much my children loved their father who'd diapered them at night when they were small, made breakfast for them every morning, and listened attentively to their stories? I couldn't help experiencing my husband through my daughters. I felt connected to him by their love, even when I myself felt most alone.

Jack felt the same way.

To be truthful, it wasn't only the children that linked us. A marriage begins with two people, but studies show that isolated couples are most vulnerable to divorce. If love remains static, it often dies, perhaps of starvation. What happened in our case was that, over the years, our small circle of love grew like a snowball rolling downhill, encompassing not only our children, but friends, old college roommates, members of our church, neighbors, and even our baby-sitters who grew up and invited us to their weddings.

Our marriage consisted of more than two people, or even four. It was made up of our love of nature, the couples who were our extended family, our fascination with astronomy, our involvement with social causes, the thousand-and-one threads from which we'd woven the fabric of our lives. How could we tear it to shreds unless there were absolutely no other way to fix things? There was more at stake than our individual destinies, and so we hesitated, long enough to find ourselves back on the same wave-length again.

For the children's sake.

Perhaps we ought to reinstate that concept, not only as the

glue that can keep a couple together long enough to get perspective on their relationship, but as a knife sharp enough to cut through the fear and insecurity that all too often keeps women from leaving husbands who are abusive fathers.

There are times when self-interest illuminates only part of the picture, when the strength we need to keep a commitment — or to break one — resides in the love we feel for our children. We are one another's keepers, never more than when we have been given children in trust. When a child is born, the deck is stacked in a new way.

The game of solitaire is over.

June 1995

MY HUSBAND'S OLDER sister committed suicide in June 1959, while we were on our honeymoon. She was twenty-nine years old. My husband was twenty-five. Marge left a note addressed, "To my father, the only one who loved me," striking out at her mother, from whom she was estranged, and at her brother, who she was convinced had abandoned her for me.

It was the sad culmination of a series of events set in motion by our engagement. When we met, I was in awe of Marge. She'd worked on the film "War and Peace." She'd had a book review published in *Newsweek*. She was sophisticated, chic, a world traveler. She was also moody and difficult. So was I.

That may even have been the reason she had strong objections to our marriage. All I knew was I didn't want to hear them.

One night, when we were visiting her, she began telling Jack all the reasons I'd make an unsuitable wife. I ran into her bathroom to sob in private. In the morning, Marge called Jack, hurt and furious. I'd written, "I hate you!" in lipstick on a roll of toilet paper, then sat politely by Jack's side for the rest of the evening, leaving my true feelings behind in the bathroom for her to find when she least expected it.

How could I have done such a thing? The good girl I was at twenty could never have been so spiteful, or so direct. I couldn't recall having done it, but I must have. Part of me had scribbled that message while the rest of me looked the other way. The whole idea of having done something and then erased it from my memory scared me, made me wonder what other dangerous impulses of mine might take possession of me. It poisoned all our further interactions.

Marge was a bridesmaid at our wedding, but we weren't speaking.

Three weeks later, after her funeral, this is how I made sense of it all. I was merely a bit player brought on stage during the last act of a family tragedy, dragged in at the last moment to bring the whole house crashing down. No one had told me the plot, taught me my lines, or warned me that my behavior might have serious consequences. I considered myself innocent and ignorant in equal measure, more sinned against than sinning.

Still, Jack and Marge had been close all their lives, and her suicide was almost unendurable for him. I understood how much courage it took not to handle his grief by leaving me and all that pain and rage behind. I loved him, admired him, was grateful that he chose to stay married to me. And I absolutely refused to be implicated in Marge's suicide.

She was gone, to my relief, though I never said that out loud to anyone. Our enmity had been so overwhelming that I was sure we'd never have become the close friends Jack had set his heart on. Our discussions of Marge's death evolved into a set piece: She'd felt rejected by her mother. She was in competition for her father's love. She needed more reassurance than Jack had been able to give her. As for my role, the topic was off limits, dark and untouchable.

Not long ago, Jack and I attended a three-day workshop for couples at the Option Institute. It was a wonderful experience, affirming and restorative, but on our last night there, I woke at four A.M. to find Jack sitting on the edge of the bed, wide awake. When he said he'd been up half the night, I was instantly apprehensive. He wanted to talk. I held my breath.

"I don't know if you can bear to hear this, but I want you to acknowledge how much I lost when Marge died," he said.

"I know," I said. "It was terrible."

"You played a part in it," he went on. "You preferred to think of her as stronger and healthier, but she was just as insecure and vulnerable as you were. You were as provocative as she was, as much a participant as any of us. I hate your blaming everyone but yourself!"

In the darkness before dawn, I was shocked to discover that, like a stone thrown in water, the shock waves of Marge's suicide had been silently, savagely rocking our relationship for thirty-five years.

"We were in a life-and-death struggle over you," I responded, "and I did everything I could to win. I made things worse. I know I did. If it happened today, I'd do it differently, but I was hurt and frightened. I never tried to understand how Marge felt. I'm truly sorry."

The admission I'd dreaded came as a relief, releasing the pain that denial always brings. I discovered I could acknowledge the hurtful young woman I'd been and take responsibility for what she'd done, without hating her or feeling she was forever unworthy of love.

As a thin wisp of light beneath the shade signaled the coming of dawn, Jack and I finally let Marge die.

September 1997

LET ME TELL YOU
a story about a king and a queen.

One evening, when he was feeling romantic, the king asked his wife, "My dearest darling, whom do love most in all the world?" He was sure, of course, that his name would come to her lips. The queen hesitated briefly, afraid of all the power her husband possessed, but in the end she decided to tell the truth.

"You know, my dear," she replied, "I love myself most."

After a long moment's thought, the king replied, "Well, now that I think of it, I love myself the most, too."

I laughed out loud when I first heard that tale, probably because it breaks one of our last cultural taboos. This royal couple gives voice to the one thing lovers dare not say to one other, and yet unarguably, this king and queen speak the truth. No matter how passionately we profess our love for others, we invariably put ourselves and our own feelings first.

Although we believe that love should enhance the well-being of both partners, we keep a running tally to make sure we get our share. We look out for our own interests — if we don't, who will? Yet when those who have sworn undying love for us do the exact same thing, we're disappointed. The idea that love means that two individuals will place the good of the other above their own is an illusion we cherish, even as the divorce rates soar.

It's simply not possible to enact movie love scenes our whole life long. Yet lovers, dreaming of long-stemmed roses, passionate letters, and the electric shock of the other's touch, give very little thought to what comes next in a relationship besides boredom. There is another kind of love worth cherishing, a satisfying and fulfilling life after infatuation, but it requires trading in "I love you more than life itself" for reality. It requires an appreciation of "Next to myself, I love you best."

I recently read in one of my husband's psychiatric journals that most failed marriages have, at some point in their history, an identifiable turning point, a defining moment when one partner asked the other for help and was refused or let down. That act of abandonment and betrayal erodes love and trust and begins to define the relationship: *I turned to you and you turned away. How can I know you love me if you won't put my needs first?* The irony, of course, is that the needy one is also putting his or her needs first.

We have to learn not to expect too much of one another.

Take my case. I have been ill with shingles almost a month now, in so much pain I could barely feed and bathe myself. I'm confident my husband would have given me his undivided love and attention in every spare moment if it hadn't been golf season . . .

He had a date to play golf in Vermont with old friends.

I didn't ask Jack to cancel his plans because I knew he couldn't make my ordeal any easier. Loving myself best, I made sure I could manage without him. Loving Jack second best, I sent him off as cheerfully as I could under the circumstances. Jack actually offered to cancel his plans, but loving himself best, he clearly wanted to go. Loving me second best, he would have sacrificed his golf game if I'd stated clearly that it was really important to me.

In the end I didn't ask and Jack didn't insist on staying. He played golf and I survived. What more can two people expect of each other?

I wasn't angry because, after thirty-five years of marriage, I assume it's my responsibility to ask clearly for what I want. I've given up wishing that Jack could read my mind. He has trouble enough deciphering the spoken word. Nor do I demand that my husband be enthusiastic when giving up his wishes in order to accommodate mine. How can I resent his reluctance when in my heart I'd feel exactly the same way? Given that selfishness is hard-wired in our species as a survival mechanism, there are no sweeter words than, "If I had my way, I wouldn't choose to do this. But I love you, so I will."

It's a miracle we're capable of as much devotion as we are.

Marriage, like all of life, is a place where people look out for themselves, but here's the irony: It's in our own interest to care deeply about meeting our partner's needs. True love means knowing that the best way to take care of ourselves is to care for others.

By the way, the king and queen did live happily ever after.

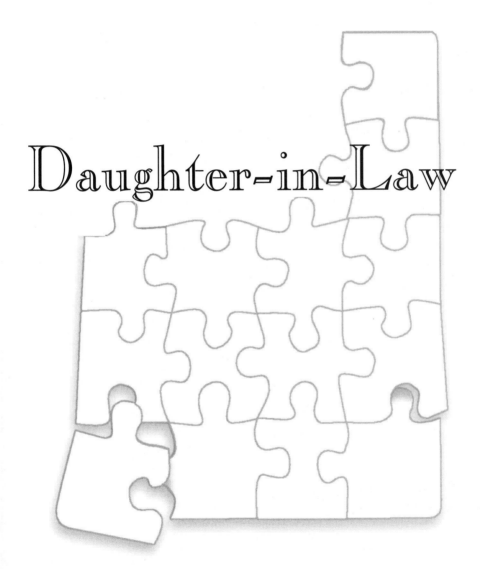

Daughter-in-Law

BERT, MY MOTHER-IN-LAW, just left after a five-day visit, and I am anything but peaceful. Some feeling I can't put my finger on is rattling around inside me, making me irritable and restless. A vague feeling of unease is ruining my sleep at night and keeping everyone at arm's length during the day.

I need to think about what happened.

I don't want to make a defeat out of a victory, so let me say now: The visit went better than I could ever have dreamed.

All the house cleaning and grocery shopping and food preparation I did the week before Bert arrived paid off. She loved the raspberries from our garden that I served in the ceramic basket she'd given us, the cheese pie I resurrected from her old recipe, the scallops in cheese sauce I served in the seashells that once were hers. She liked our friends and welcomed them as they came for breakfast, lunch, and dinner in a steady stream. She was a good sport about getting her first massage from a friend of ours, and she's the only person I know, including me, who watched without complaint the hours of old family movies we recently put on videotape. She even praised our dog.

She was a warm and appreciative guest. It's just that this is only the second time in twenty-eight years that she's spent a night in our house.

Last summer was the first.

My mother-in-law is not a communicative person, but I felt compelled to bring up our troubled history when she told her favorite story again — how her mother-in-law, who'd welcomed her into the family with open arms, had rebuked someone who'd referred to Bert as her daughter-in-law. "She said to this woman, 'She's my daughter now,' " my mother-in-law repeated with obvious pride.

I know she isn't deliberately trying to hurt me each time she tells this story, but my eyes filled with tears. I couldn't keep silent any longer.

"Don't you feel bad that you haven't come to visit before this?" I asked, conscious of her eighty-five years and the fact that she now needs assistance to make it to our second-floor guest room.

In reply, she blamed her husband's ten-year losing battle with Alzheimer's Disease.

"But even before that," I said, unable to let it go.

"Well, you and I got off on the wrong foot," she replied at last.

I had to be satisfied with that.

The problem is I can't forget those years and how much I hoped to be welcomed into my husband's family. When my in-laws asked us to postpone our wedding date, I remember my mother asking, "What can they object to, Linda? You're Jewish, you went to college, and your dental work is paid for." My in-laws' only explanation was that they felt their twenty-six-year-old son, still in medical school, was too young.

I added two and two. They didn't like me.

They didn't seem to like my parents, either, and despite Bert's impeccable manners, she never sent a thank-you note for my father's oddball gifts to them, a king-size bottle of cod liver oil, which was his favorite elixir, and what was then a new-fangled Polaroid camera. After the wedding, twenty years went by with absolutely no contact between the two families. How could I blame my in-laws for their unfriendliness when my folks were so different from them? How could I help but resent them out of loyalty to my own parents?

We got off on two wrong feet.

I've tried to dwell on how little my in-laws have interfered in our lives and how generous they've been financially. But this past weekend, when my mother-in-law dropped a ceramic pitcher my husband and I had brought back from Ireland, I couldn't help but remember when Laura, who was two at the time, broke an inexpensive clay turtle Bert had purchased in Mexico. My mother-in-law had been so upset she decided that our children, her only grandchildren, wouldn't be allowed back into her house until they were old enough to be more careful with her belongings.

Twenty years later I found myself reassuring my mother-in-law that the broken pitcher was unimportant, but I couldn't help thinking how different things might have been if only she could have foreseen that some day she might be the one who wouldn't be able to hold on to a fragile object.

If only . . .

Are there two more pointless words in the English language? We got off to a terrible start.

It took my father-in-law's death, I think, to show my mother-in-law that she needed all the love she could gather in this world, and that she'd been needlessly cutting herself off from the people who could be there for her when she needed them.

When it came time to leave, Bert whispered to me, "I've come to love you so much," and my heart lurched in my chest as I pressed my lips against the parchment of her cheeks. I remembered with what longing I had once said to this woman, "Some day we'll have a son to carry on your name," and how she'd replied disapprovingly, "Not soon, I hope."

That's how it is. The past intersects the present, like over-lapping images on the screen of my consciousness. How can I help but respond to my mother-in-law's loneliness and need? How can I keep from recalling the years of my own hurt and disappointment?

What comes to mind is a phrase I've adapted from Ken Keyes' book *Prescription for Happiness*: When in confusion, turn up your love.

January 1990

"LINDA, DON'T YOU THINK it's time to leave for the airport?" my mother-in-law asked on the last day of our visit to Florida.

"Not really," I said. "Who wants to spend a beautiful sunny afternoon sitting at an airport? We have plenty of time."

"I know I always get places too early," she persisted, "but there's always the possibility you'll be held up at the train crossing." My mother-in-law recited a list of events that might spell disaster, but she saved her best rationale for last. "After all, isn't it better to arrive a little early than to miss your plane entirely?"

How could I argue with the voice of caution? My husband and I might be held up by a train or have trouble returning our rented car. We might take a wrong turn, be sideswiped by an elderly driver, or break a leg running up the ramp. There's no end to the possible misfortunes that might befall us. Who can deny that? I certainly wasn't willing to kiss the money we'd paid for our plane tickets good-bye, either, and so I capitulated and rushed my husband out the door. Later I had plenty of time to think. We arrived an hour early for a plane that ended up leaving an hour late.

I can't argue with her reasoning. Who can say, yes, I want to miss my plane add end up stranded in Florida? The world is full of words to the wise, all saying: *Take care, take care!*

Who wants to be thought a fool for ignoring them?

Yet is that any way to lead a life? It may be better to be safe than sorry, but what if you end up safe *and* sorry? What if, in acting defensively, in always anticipating the worst, you miss out on all the fun that goes with a little spontaneity? If you always focus on what you might lose, you forget what you might gain. I prefer to take my chances and deal with the consequences.

For example, my daughter Laura and son-in-law, Brian, are in the process of buying a house. The owners invited them over for brunch.

"Let me give you some advice," offered a friendly real-estate broker, when I mentioned the upcoming meeting. "The buyers should never get chummy with the sellers. You're asking for trouble."

I never did find out exactly what the danger was. Maybe that they'd get into a wrangle and ruin the deal. Or the meeting would give both parties the opportunity to pull a fast one or hate one another's guts. The people could have been hateful. They could have tried to charge extra for every little thing. Something bad could have happened. In fact, something bad can *always* happen — in any circumstance under any conditions to anyone.

Laura and Brian went anyway.

As it turned out, the two families clicked. They had careers in common, and I suspect that when the owners moved into the house twelve years ago, they were very like our kids. As a result of that meeting, the owners left behind some wonderful furniture and passed along the names of workmen. They described the neighbors, including one who baby-sits cats. Laura got a chance to shoot a roll of film so I could send pictures of the house to Bert and my parents.

Nothing spectacular, really, and yet the transaction felt more personal somehow, more satisfying. Our children had seen the house. Now they saw their future home and got a chance to experience the warmth of the dining room with sunlight streaming in the windows.

Our kids took a chance. Terrible things might have happened, but they didn't. Most of the time, they don't. That's what cautionary tales leave out.

Much of what passes for wisdom in this culture is motivated by fear. Something might go wrong. *Do it anyway.* People will cheat you. *Have faith just the same.* Never count on anyone. *Take a chance.* Expect the worst. *Don't let fear rule you.*

There aren't any guarantees, but I've learned this from Bert: Fear is a restricting emotion. It narrows your options, limits your chances, constricts your life. It imprisons you in a world full of dangers. It keeps you from seeing the exciting possibilities right before your eyes. To be alive, after all, is to be at risk.

I think of Gerald Jampolsky's book *Love Is Letting Go of Fear.*

You can say the same about life.

February 1990

MY FATHER-IN-LAW had come down with pneumonia four years after he'd been admitted with Alzheimer's Disease to a nursing home. It had been his second bout with severe pneumonia, a disease which, in an age of fewer medical miracles, was called the "old man's friend." With my mother-in-law's consent, George had been rushed to the hospital and brought back from death's door a second time. It was at this point that my husband and his mom had reflected on the quality of life my father-in-law was being rescued for, and the two of them had decided against any more heroic measures.

George never got pneumonia again. Instead, unable to do any

of the things we consider part of the human repertoire — speaking, walking, recognizing people he loved — he had survived for another three years.

We had known my father-in-law had no desire to live once his mental faculties were gone. He'd announced to my husband that he wanted to take his own life when the first symptoms of Alzheimer's appeared, but one day he crossed a border in his mind from which he was unable to return, and from then on, his fate had rested in hands other than his own. That responsibility had weighed heavily on my mother-in-law. Who of us would ever wish to choose the moment of death for someone we love?

As I grow older, I see this scenario again and again: a parent of one of my friends becomes seriously ill, leaving the remaining partner to determine which is most desirable — a continuance of a damaged life, or death. That's why, on a snowy Sunday afternoon two weeks ago, I sat entranced, watching Frederick Wiseman's documentary "Near Death" on PBS. What I saw was hardly reassuring. Filmed in a hospital's intensive care unit, most of the families shown seemed never to have previously considered the possibility of dying.

At first, they attempt to deny reality, acting as if stronger medication and painful procedures are the only possible means to express their love and concern. A dying woman appears to accept a tracheotomy because she is worried about her husband's ability to cope with her loss. Family members reportedly say, "Don't cause any suffering, but do everything you can," failing to recognize that those options are often incompatible.

Is this the way it has to be? Must the last words spoken to a terminal patient be lies? Must men or women die without being given a chance to say a meaningful word to those left behind?

The doctors compare notes about when each family "will be ready to hear" the bad news. They slowly ease these grief-stricken families toward the truth, hoping they will see that death is the only possible healing. But in this film, the realization that death is near often comes too late.

"Charley's my life," a woman cries. We hear her, but Charley is unconscious, beyond her reach. The real tragedy of this story is that when Charley first sensed he was dying, all he could share with his wife was his fear that he was going crazy. I don't understand what kept these two silent and apart, but I see the high price they paid for their denial. It is terrible to be denied the opportunity to say good-bye.

Every once in a while my husband and I talk about our deaths. My husband leans toward theories of reincarnation. I believe my soul molecules will go back into some great undifferentiated spirit pool, the way bodies rejoin the chemical composition of earth. We've drawn up our wills, discussed how to dispose of our bodies, and promised each other to make sure our last hours will be free of pain. We don't find the topic unpleasant. In fact, our life together never seems more precious than when we acknowledge its fragility.

The year we decided to be cremated, we told our kids, who thought we were crazy. It became a family joke that Jack and I were searching for an urn for our ashes. Eventually we did find a large, hand-thrown piece of pottery that suited our purpose. It sounds strange, but I like keeping it on the sideboard in our dining room and knowing that eventually all of us, including the dog, will be together again.

Jack and I have also made out living wills. They make absolutely clear that, in case of terminal illness, medication is to be mercifully administered, even if it shortens our lives. We've given copies to our children and our doctor. I carry a card in my wallet with the phone number of a support group called Concern for Dying. If I ever have to make a decision for myself or a family member, I'll be able to seek help from people who've dealt with these issues before.

It doesn't feel morbid to talk about this. It's only when we bury the fear of death so deep that we never touch it that we give it ultimate power over us. I'd rather think about dying now than be panicked into a bad decision later, or end up forcing someone I love to linger in pain because I'm not ready to hear the truth. I don't want my children to stand by my bedside, agonizing over what I want them to do.

Perhaps they'll agonize anyway, but I'll know I've done my very best to make it clear that I'm not afraid of the last gift a merciful God gives the living.

MY MOTHER-IN-LAW may be dying at home in Florida. It's hard to tell from this distance. Her nurses make frantic phone calls to my husband, while the doctor keeps his own counsel. "There's no way of knowing," he says. "I really can't say." As a result, my husband's made three impromptu trips in the last six weeks, but by the time he arrives, his mother is better and on the road to recovery.

Not surprisingly, she's also tremendously glad to see him.

I think of her lying in bed alone, surrounded by nurses she's never met before, and I can't help but imagine myself in her place. I know I don't want to die without someone by my side who can respond to the particular person I am. If her tangled web of symptoms isn't straightened out, it's possible my mother-in-law will be surrounded by strangers at the end of her life. How did we arrive at this place? What decisions led us all into this dreadful situation?

I need to know in order to avoid making the same mistakes.

My in-laws, when they were our age, were part of a tightly knit group on Long Island, one of eight couples who met to play cards every Friday night for twenty years. Between hands, they asked after each other's kids, consulted on domestic problems, and kept track of mutual acquaintances. Perhaps because my husband's parents were both only children, Jack called his parents' friends "Aunt" and "Uncle." They certainly felt like relatives to him.

Still, when the time came to retire, none of them took into consideration their connection to one another. They each had their favorite Southern location, chosen for its cultural activities, its shopping, or its coastline. They assumed that keeping in touch would take care of itself, never dreaming that, as they aged, the ties they'd forged over a lifetime would quickly unravel.

It never seems to have occurred to any of them that they were one another's most valuable hedge against old age, or that having one another close at hand would be more beneficial to their final years than a well-equipped clubhouse. For the most part, we don't think of ourselves as existing in a human context that's essential to our survival. We talk about "uprooting" ourselves, but only

metaphorically. When my father-in-law, George, got Alzheimers'
within months of moving away from everything that gave his life
meaning — his home, his garden, his family and friends — I
couldn't push away the image that came to mind: He reminded me
of a cut flower shriveling in a vase.

My father-in law was in no condition to travel, and so for years
my husband visited Florida every six weeks, with a child in tow. He
resisted his parents' suggestion that he go into practice in the
Sunshine State. When George entered a nursing home, Bert put
her life on hold. With no old friends to support her, it was a trying
watch of eight empty years. It wasn't until her husband died that
she decided she wanted to visit us in Marblehead, and we worked
on healing the rift that had arisen when I fell in love with her son.

She seemed satisfied to remain in Florida, though she spoke
constantly of her loneliness. Then we discovered that she'd had
several serious falls. Once, when the alarm around her neck failed,
she lay on the floor until the cleaning lady showed up for work the
next day.

This past winter we located a supported living situation for
the elderly near our home where she'd have a large room of her own,
meals, and kitchen privileges. My husband suggested that she
move closer to us, but she insisted she wasn't ready. She'd consider
it when she could no longer take care of herself.

We went along with her wishes, but I realize now we were all
harboring an illusion, one in which her decline would be progres-
sive, predictable, and manageable. Last month's sudden operation,
which had to be repeated when the stitches tore, wreaked havoc
with our best-laid plans. Despite my husband's visits, she's on her
own, and we're helpless at this distance to console or comfort her.
She has no one else.

For some reason people find it difficult to entertain the possibility of illness when they're well, of limitation when they're whole,
of dependence when they're doing just fine, thank you, on their
own. My mother-in-law always postponed activities with the phrases
"until I'm stronger" or "once I get my energy back," and I never felt
I had permission to dash such a lovely fantasy with a painful truth,
like "Bert, you're going to meet Julie's fiancé now or never."

Because we couldn't talk, there are now fifteen hundred miles between us, though I suspect that's not what any of us really wanted.

I like to think my husband and I will do it differently, that we'll be fearless in the face of our own destiny. We may choose to spend part of the winters in a warmer place, but I want to die in the town where we raised our children, built our friendships, and are part of the community. If we start making thoughtless choices, I hope someone will take this column and wave it in my face.

I stayed alert to welcome my children into this world.

I want them near me when it's time to say farewell.

November 1991

MY MOTHER-IN-LAW is finally coming to stay in a nursing home near our house, and I'm looking forward to it. This is remarkable for the following reason: When my husband's older sister, Marge, her only other child, committed suicide while Jack and I were on our honeymoon, she held our marriage, and me in particular, responsible.

We never discussed the subject. The early years of our polite and distant relationship were strained enough without a confrontation. Once Jack and I had children, however, our toddlers were far too lively for her and so — at my instigation and with her happy agreement — Jack began visiting his parents without me, one child at a time. Bert and I had almost no contact until my daughters left for college. I sent her copies of the weekly letters I wrote them, and she sent word through Jack that she appreciated them.

Perhaps my letters had an effect, or perhaps she realized that Jack and I were all that was left of her family. Whatever the reason, after her husband died five years ago, my mother-in-law, in an abrupt about-face, expressed a wish to visit us. Even worse, my husband wanted me to accept his mother's overture with an open heart.

I didn't think I could do it.

In the first place, childish as this is, I resented that my husband and children had always enjoyed their time with Grandma Bert in Florida because it made me the only one still holding her accountable for the crimes she'd committed against me. Since I was the only one keeping score, I was reluctant to let her off the hook. If I forgave her, she'd end up getting off scot-free in this life. Where was justice if this woman were allowed to erase the events of twenty years without even so much as an "I'm sorry"?

In addition, I no longer felt an obligation to be a good daughter-in-law. The word "should" lost its power over me when I came to see that, as much as we believe we do things we don't want to because we "should," we must want to or we wouldn't do them. In my own life, I've gone to great pains to rule out, "I have to do this and I hate it," in favor of "If I'm going to do this, I have to take responsibility for the fact that I must want to at some level."

If I was going to have Bert back in my life, I was determined to make it a positive experience.

I wasn't willing to fake it — not that my mother-in-law would know the difference. At the mere thought of burying my feelings, I could feel a migraine coming on. I saw only two happy choices. My mother-in-law would settle near us and be visited by other family members. Or I'd happily join the team caring for her.

Unfortunately, before she came, I had to figure out how to take down the wall I had so painstakingly built between us, judgment by judgment, brick upon brick.

Why did something that had happened so many years ago still hurt so much now? What was keeping those resentments alive? If an unhappy woman had unfairly blamed me for her daughter's death, why did that make me unhappy? I knew the answer: *Because my husband hadn't stood up to her.* All right, he hadn't forced her to accept me or broken off his relationship with her to protect me. Why would that make me unhappy? *Because in my heart, no matter how many times he denied it, I believed he loved his mother more than he loved me.* Every time I accused him, he swore it wasn't true, but for all the years of our marriage, every time his mother came into my thoughts, every time her name entered the conversation, I felt that insult anew, as if someone were twisting a knife one notch deeper into my heart.

Taking a look at those beliefs with a therapist, I saw something that hadn't occurred to me before: Perhaps what made my husband so attentive to his mother was his strong sense of duty, a trait I loved and admired in its other guises. Wasn't it possible that love kept him at my side while loyalty to his mom motivated him to be such an attentive son? That shift in perspective brought with it an enormous flood of relief, which left me feeling so much better. Taking a deep breath, I searched for the pain I'd been carrying around all these years. Like a miracle, the knife I'd been twisting was nowhere to be found.

At last I felt that there was no evil intention in my sister-in-law's suicide or my mother-in-law's rejection, just too much unhappiness to be borne in silence or in secret. I gave up keeping score like a vengeful umpire. That is a role for those who are still in pain.

This move gives me the opportunity to make peace with a difficult old lady before she reaches the end of her journey.

I plan to take it.

January 1992

THIS IS MY MORNING to write, so I have brought a pencil and paper to the nursing home where I sit by my mother-in-law as she struggles to breathe. Her cough has turned out to be a symptom of congestive heart failure. None of us knows how much longer Bert will live.

Since she arrived from Florida three months ago, her room has been a family gathering place. I'm content to be here with her, and I think she takes some comfort from my presence. In the early years of my marriage, I often imagined myself taking an occasion such as this to confront her with what I then supposed would be my undying animosity, but now I feel only compassion as well as a great sadness. The woman I once resented so intensely is not this tiny figure swallowed up in the upholstered arms of an oversized chair. My enemy has departed and in her place is an even-tempered soul who praises her nurses and lights up when her great-granddaughter appears.

My husband and two daughters have always loved her. I found that hard to understand for she was always very strict and never physically affectionate. She didn't take her grandchildren to the park, read them bedtime stories, or make an effort to get to know them. She banished my babies from her house to protect her possessions.

Still, they came to care about her. During their visits, my children came to see qualities in her that were invisible to me. They overlooked her shortcomings because they felt connected to her. Where I saw a lack of caring, they experienced her loving presence.

I don't understand why I am beginning to cry.

I think I got love wrong somewhere along the way. I've never been able to imagine anyone loving me without my first having done something to deserve it. I give my granddaughter a bottle (Bert never did that) and think, *When she is older, I'll matter to her.* I write weekly letters to my child at college (Bert never did that) and think, *Some day Julie will remember how much effort I poured into loving her.* I once asked my dad if he loved me, and he responded by asking, "What have you done to deserve it?" I think I took his question too much to heart. It has hung like a poisonous shadow over every relationship.

This is what I say to myself: *If love is a payment for services rendered, I've put in the necessary hours. If love is a reward for good behavior, I can recite a list of my good deeds.* Sitting here, watching my mother-in-law's gnarled fingers tighten in rhythm with her troubled breathing, I see another truth I cannot push away: *All my efforts to earn love may be utterly beside the point.*

I always thought you had to earn love in order to receive it. I fought for that belief with every judgment I could muster because it frightened me that love could slip out of my control. I took comfort from, "You owe me." I created the illusion of safety by believing certain acts would guarantee me an eventual payback.

I was wrong.

All around us is the evidence that there are no guarantees. And few of us, experiencing the gift of another's love, do not feel in some portion of our soul, *This is more than I deserve.*

I have been privileged to catch sight of a great mystery in this room where a worn-out heart perseveres. Perhaps love is always unmerited, is never a reward for performance. The love my children feel for their grandmother shows me that the power that opens one's heart or draws forth the love of another cannot be programmed or controlled.

Though we act as if love is ours to distribute as we please, it flows through us like a wild river with a will of its own. Disregarding resolutions and obligations, it digs its own channels, compelling our consent. Love may be the human counterpart of gravity, that awesome power which holds the galaxies together. Arising spontaneously within us, it binds us to one another, disdaining justification or cause. In the end, it may be that all we can really count on is one another's generosity of spirit.

I find reassurance in my mother-in-law's fate, in the promise that the love my family feels for me does not depend on how much I do for them. I must learn to trust in love that is freely given.

Over the years Bert has been my nemesis and my rival. This morning she is my teacher.

July 1992

THIS HAS BEEN THE busiest week of my life. Once-in-a-lifetime events took place faster than I could assimilate them. Before I could even begin to fashion a response to one, I had to cope with the next.

I'm left with a series of jarring images: the quiet jubilation of my mother-in-law's ninetieth birthday party; Bert desperately gasping for breath only twenty-four hours later; my younger daughter in a fitting room, slipping into her wedding gown; Bert's coffin sinking into her grave in the afternoon sunlight; a Fourth of July parade; a house full of guests; a party in full swing in the rain; a small package on the porch containing the ashes of our dog.

Those were the highlights. This is the rundown.

My daughter Julie and her fiancé, Chris, flew up from South Carolina on Friday, a week before their wedding. That afternoon, four generations of Weltners posed in the sunny nursing home garden for a formal portrait, our birthday gift to Bert. On Saturday night, two old friends of Bert's, who had flown in from Florida and California, came to her birthday party, and as we said good-bye, Bert's friend Natalie pleaded with me, "Don't make her attend the wedding, Linda. She doesn't think she has the strength." On Monday morning, as Julie and I began to tackle the last of the last-minute wedding preparations, my mother-in-law went into a sudden decline.

I'll always remember my granddaughter, Jessie, full of energy at sixteen months, running full-tilt in the nursing home garden while her great-grandmother struggled to breathe. My husband was holding his mother's hand when she died, just as I had cradled our dog's head in my lap as his life ended exactly one week earlier. Bert died on Tuesday, and on Thursday our extended family made the fifteen-hour round-trip journey by car to the cemetery in upper New York state where Bert's husband and daughter are buried. Jack conducted a graveside ceremony.

In between, Julie and Chris dashed to meetings with the minister, the florist, the organist, the jeweler, the hairdresser, and heaven-knows-who, handling the disruption of their plans with such grace that I felt totally relieved of responsibility. I joined them just once, long enough to catch a dazzling glimpse of my daughter, gowned and glowing, multiplied endlessly in a dressing room's triple mirrors.

On the next Friday afternoon, I kept my promise and taught a writing workshop at the Marblehead Arts Festival. That evening, my brother and his family arrived for the holiday weekend. On Saturday morning, we all marched in the neighborhood Fourth of July parade. Julie and I wore costumes I'd found at a yard sale. She was a cardboard tube of toothpaste to match my cardboard toothbrush. My niece, Sarah, two, waddled along in a ballerina costume while my nephew, Sam, four, wore baseball pajamas. Jack led the procession, boldly attempting to play the same song as the rest of the band on his battered tuba. Then my neighbor Fred Kraybill and I ran the kids' games, as we have for the past fifteen years. That afternoon, my daughter Laura and Brian's annual Fourth of July party took place in our yard. When it rained, the house filled to the brim with their friends.

The first lull in the action came that evening. I stepped outside for a moment of quiet and noticed that a small package had been placed by our back door. The vet had sent over our dog Buckwheat's ashes.

As the past week's images flashed and overlapped in my mind, everything seemed lit with a glow even the rain couldn't extinguish. I experienced myself as a link in the chain of generations that has maintained our neighborhood's elaborate Fourth of July celebration since the early 1900s. The essays in my writing workshop seemed miraculously heartfelt. Julie's wedding beckoned just over the horizon. I felt carried along by the voluminous flow of people and events.

I was overcome by the richness of my life.

Two deaths testified to the inevitability of endings, not only to the ending of individual lives, but also to the end of my own energy and enthusiasm and satisfaction. For a brief moment, the shadow of their passing made me ecstatically conscious of my aliveness, as if living in a state of finite possibilities made each one precious beyond measure.

I looked up at the display of stars in the dark expanse of cloudless sky, trembling, as if I too were a burning sun, glittering in the night.

July 1992

"ARE YOU SURE you want to mention your mother-in-law's death in the same column as the dog's?" my editor asked me.

An acquaintance put it more strongly: "How could you write about the death of a person and the death of a dog as if they were comparable?"

My brother felt the same discomfort about my mother's fate. "It's bad enough that you've put Buckwheat's ashes in with

Mom's," Ken said, gesturing toward the pottery urn on our dining room sideboard, "but how could you put Buck's collar around the urn? It's insulting to Mom, don't you think?"

No, I don't.

How does the love given to one being diminish the love we feel for another? How does my attachment to my dog, who was my close companion all his life, adversely affect my love for my mother or my mother-in-law? If I'd never cared for Buck, could I have taken that unused portion of love and redistributed it, like an extra piece of pie? Or does one love to the limits of one's capacity for loving in every instance?

For the sake of argument, though, let's say it's important to know whom I loved best in the deepest recesses of my heart. How would I measure that? Is there an official listing of love objects, rated from the most deserving to the least, that I'm morally obligated to follow? Or is love actually independent of all its objects, a statement instead of the lover's depth and strength of feeling?

And though this is quite a stretch, bear with me for one more question. Is there a possibility that, in order for the human race to survive, each of us must enlarge the scope of our loving until it moves beyond our own species to encompass the entire planet, not only animals and plants, but even that which the Western world considers non-living?

I ask because my husband and I have been puzzling over the Buddha's teaching in the Diamond Sutra that there is no meaningful distinction between living and non-living beings. "What we call non-living makes what we call living beings possible. If we destroy the non-living, we also destroy the living," writes Thich Nhat Hanh in his book *The Diamond that Cuts through Illusion*. Without soil, there would be no plants to eat; without oxygen, no air to breathe. Without rocks, we would sink into volcanic fire. Without water, we could not exist. A spider's web and the silkworm's cocoon emerge from living creatures. These "things" are an essential part of the living world, just as fingernails and bone are part of a living body.

It is only our tendency to conceptualize, to separate wholeness into its component parts, that leads us to imagine discontinuity where there is connection, interdependence, and a progression of stages. Only one heartbeat separates the living from the non-living, as death proves again and again. Was the dog I carried into the vet's more like or more different from the creature I cradled after his death? Or is what we call "living" just a single phase in a much longer process whose beginning and end are beyond our rational understanding?

David Spangler, author of *The Rebirth of the Sacred*, writes, "The recognition of life within the earth is the recognition that, in fact, there is nothing that is not living. Therefore you may enter into a reciprocal relationship with everything." He goes on to say that, in a world in which some things are deemed unworthy of a loving response, forests, oceans, air — and eventually human beings — are diminished, turned into objects designed merely for use. In a world where the assumption of life means an assumption of sacredness, only a "living" planet becomes deserving of our protection and preservation.

I am hardly an enlightened being, but the path I am traveling leads to more loving, not less. In this last generative stage of my life, I want to become wise enough to see and enter into relationship with the luminous essence that dwells in all of God's creation.

Once, during a visit to Wyoming, I chose to see the grandeur of the Tetons as a reflection of its inner spirit rather than as a projection of my own mind. I can only report that, upon opening myself to this possibility, those snowy peaks seemed to speak to me, soul to soul, proclaiming our connection.

I have been privileged to be present at the moment of death twice this month, and what I have taken from the experience is this: The animating life force that mysteriously vanishes at the end of our days seemed exactly the same in both cases. I have come to believe this single life force enters into an infinite variety of forms, awakening flesh and blood, fur and feather, shell and carapace, leaf and petal, in ways that are visible to us. I am willing to consider that life also quickens around us in ways we do not recognize, but which were once known intuitively by seers and primitive people. Scientists someday may prove what some only hypothesize now: All these seemingly separate living and "non-living" forms make up one living planet that many call Gaia.

Some things, as well as some people, call to me more power-fully than others, of course, but that doesn't mean I can't try, in every case, to love as deeply as possible. I take courage from the Chassidic philosopher Rabbi Manis Friedman, who was asked how in the world he found enough love within himself for all fourteen of his children.

"My love doesn't divide," he replied. "It only multiplies."

BEFORE MY MOTHER-IN-LAW had entered the nursing home, she had allowed us to pack up and bring her most treasured possessions North. There were two sets of English china, crystal glasses, and lovely bone china figurines my daughters had admired for years, silver serving pieces, and a teacup collection. There were also the gifts her husband had been given on his thirtieth anniversary with Paramount Pictures, objects care-fully chosen by Paramount officials around the world especially for the occasion.

We had hired a Florida moving company to pack up her treasures, and we had sent the boxes insured with UPS. My husband had felt uncomfortable using or displaying any of his mother's things while she was still alive, so when they arrived, we had them carried up to our attic to store them until Bert died.

I understood his compunctions. Bert's possessions seemed to be the embodiment of her whole life. She'd shopped for them, displayed them, guarded them, poured her life's energy into caring for them. Bert's belongings had been extensions of herself and no one else had been allowed to touch them. When she had become frail, she'd preferred they collect dust rather than be cleaned by anyone else. When my daughters had gotten married, she hadn't been able to part with the china she'd promised them — a dozen of everything in perfect condition — so the girls had selected other patterns for their bridal register. They had understood that Bert's possessions were the beloved companions of her old age.

The Thanksgiving after she died, when our whole family was together, we finally brought the boxes down from the attic. A hush fell as the first plate was removed, its broken pieces rattling in white butcher's paper. I watched as fragments emerged from the wrappings. Six crystal goblets . . . shattered. Figurines . . . beheaded. The dancing lady in the lace dress made of china . . . a crush of frilly white shards. Cups, plates, and bowls. All were cracked and chipped.

The same thing had happened to my father-in-law's retirement gifts. An elaborate carving made from an African elephant tusk . . . broken. Dolphin bookends made of Steuben glass . . . finless. An ebony elephant carved in Sudan . . . ear gone. Iridescent glass vials from Greece, reclaimed from the floor of the Mediterranean sea . . . smashed to pieces. All in all, more than a third of the shipment was destroyed.

"I hope Grandma Bert isn't watching," Julie whispered. My husband began videotaping the unpacking, documenting the damage.

"Thank God we're covered by insurance," my husband said.

But the man from UPS informed us that their insurance covered our belongings for only nine months after shipping. Besides, he said, UPS wouldn't have given us a cent at any time. The boxes, he informed us, had been improperly packed, clearly the moving company's fault.

We sent the moving company a copy of the videotape. The owner gave us the same song and dance. His insurance, too, covered breakage for only nine months. The boxes must have been thrown off the side of a truck to cause that much breakage, he insisted. It was UPS' fault.

"I can't believe my mother-in-law's most prized possessions are ruined, and no one will take responsibility," I moaned.

The mover softened. "Listen, the carrier always says it's the mover's fault, and the mover always says it's the carrier's fault. That's the way it goes. I'm real sorry your insurance lapsed, but you're caught between a rock and hard place."

I hung up, sick at heart. No matter how many times I said to myself, "They're only objects," I was drowning in remorse.

How could my husband and I, in one fell swoop, have wiped out the personal effects it had taken his mother a lifetime to collect? Why hadn't we thought to check the mover's credentials? It was shameful that my husband and I had proved such easy marks. We'd been ignorant and naïve, assuming we were indefinitely insured when we'd actually left ourselves unprotected. What kind of fools would pay over six hundred dollars to have their possessions destroyed?

Our kind, obviously.

There wasn't anything of Bert's that I wanted for myself, but we'd deprived our daughters of things they'd loved all their lives. We'd severed our children's link to their past, though they didn't seem to blame us. Every time I glimpsed the wreckage strewn around our living room, I was furious at myself all over again. My chest constricted until I could barely breathe. I couldn't seem to come to terms with what had happened.

Then I talked with my friend Maria.

"Think of Bert as an Egyptian queen, laid to rest with all the trappings of her life," she counseled. "Her things were never meant to come to you. They've gone to keep her spirit company."

It was a strangely comforting thought. Instead of being filled with regret at having irretrievably spoiled everything, perhaps everything had worked out just as Fate intended.

Given our troubled history, perhaps as Bert might have preferred it.

October 1993

AT BERT'S REQUEST, we kept her apartment in Florida for one year before selling it. When we sold it last month, Jack and I flew down to Florida to decide what to do with all the ordinary stuff — furniture and linens and kitchenware — she'd accumulated in ninety years. After three days, Jack went back to Marblehead. I stayed in Bert's apartment for another twenty-four hours, tying up loose ends. I couldn't sleep.

By midnight I'd thumbed through dozens of albums. Most of the faces were unfamiliar. I put them in a "keeper's" pile, though I doubted Jack and I would ever look at them again. I found every single one of my weekly letters carefully stored in a drawer. I threw them in the trash, counting on my descendants having too full a life to ever find time to read them. There was something about being in Bert's space that made me feel it was a lot more important to live life than to remember it.

About one-thirty I came across a suitcase full of Bert's diaries in the back of the hall closet. My heart lurched. I'd been searching for some glimpse of my mother-in-law from the beginning. Would there be a message from her at last?

By two o'clock I was no wiser than before. Bert kept very detailed records of every hotel she and her husband ever stayed in when they traveled, but her son's marriage to me — and her daughter's suicide — weren't even mentioned. My name didn't appear. I would have liked to have known how Bert truly felt about family matters, no matter what she said about me, but obviously she wasn't an introspective person, even in private. I felt exhausted by all the unfinished business in this ransacked apartment.

By two-thirty I was completely overwhelmed by the sheer magnitude of her stuff. I'd arranged umpteen drinking glasses, radios, scarves, sheets, towels, cigarette lighters, bar accessories, vases, serving trays, TVs, gloves, shoes, and candy dishes by category. They sat in clumps, looking like aimless herds of small animals. Where did this compulsion to duplicate come from? Is there no such thing as ever having enough? I was glad I'd asked a group that helps recovering addicts get settled in apartments to come by in the morning and take everything usable.

The day before a dealer had dismissed most of the paintings and knickknacks, saying, "People don't want this kind of stuff anymore." Despite the fact that I was one of those people, Jack and I had agreed we'd take most of the furniture. We had plans to insulate our living room, which we've closed off in past winters, and use it year round again. The living room would be entirely filled with Bert's furniture, though I would never have chosen any of it myself. When the moving van arrived in Marblehead, I was thinking of stretching out on my living room floor, like one of the characters in the Salem Witch Trials about to be crushed to death under massive stones, and asking the movers to stack the furniture on top of me

Why was I feeling so resentful?

By three-thirty I finally figured it out. Underneath my anger, I felt so sad I wanted to curl up in a corner and cry. Though my mother-in-law and I reconciled before her death, I couldn't locate one single happy memory in her apartment. I'd been standing by the piano in that living room when a look in Bert's eyes had informed me that the dress I'd worn to her thirtieth anniversary party was too tight. I'd been lying on the sofa bed in that den, in agony with a migraine, when Bert had scolded me for setting a bowl of ice water down on her polished floor and whisked my cold towel away.

I felt remnants of her disapproval in the pillows on the beds and the cushions of the couch, triggering memories of how much I'd initially wanted Jack's family to love and accept me. Instead, Bert kept me at arm's length, tormenting me with the story of how her own mother-in-law always loved *her* like a daughter. I couldn't believe that the chair where she had been sitting when she first told me that story would be coming home with me.

I think the pain of being judged and found wanting by your in-laws is underappreciated. It was a slow-acting poison I was never able to keep from harming my marriage. I did my own rejecting, I admit that, but only after my yearnings had been smashed to bits.

I've learned a lesson from all this. Deathbed repentance and last-minute reconciliations may be better than nothing, but they don't make up for wasted years. The pain etched into memory lingers. Forgiveness, though it has the power to soften the heart, cannot undo the past.

There is no antidote for regret.

Mother

October 1987

MY BROTHER'S FIRST CHILD
is due in two weeks, and I've been
trying to think of the perfect gift.

Ken and Barbara need everything. Barbara's mother has already given the baby a ruffled bassinet, and my sister contributed a sack of sturdy overalls and shirts.

I've been trying to think of something that actually made a difference in raising my own two daughters. What would be valuable?

A baby book popped into my mind.

You know . . . those books where you record baby's first word, save baby's first curl, and list baby's shots. They're the books you write in for your first child and pretty much ignore for the rest, the books you look at twenty years later and then reproach yourself for having failed to fill in anything past your baby's first year.

I have two of them tucked away. I'd forgotten about them until the day my daughter Julie was filling out a health form for college. She needed her immunization dates, so I sent her up to find her baby book in my study.

You have to understand that Julie and I weren't getting along all that well at the time, her senior year in high school. She had a list of grievances that matched up with my hurt feelings, and though we both woke up in the morning promising ourselves to try and get along, we rarely succeeded in getting beyond mutual tolerance. This afternoon, at least, we were cooperating.

Julie thumbed through her book, which was mostly empty, confirming her belief that she'd been the overlooked second child. Of the fifteen pages set aside for recording important events, I'd written on only six, but Julie had never seen them before.

"I had a marvelous disposition, huh?" she asked, smiling.

"You sure did," I answered, careful not to throw fuel on the fire by adding the word "then."

"Slept though the night at 4 months, sat up at 6 months, played patty cake at 9 months, climbs stairs like a madwoman at 13 months."

"That's you," I said.

"Listen to the words I knew at 16 months," she said. " *'Ki-ki,' 'baby,' 'up', 'no,' 'open,' 'daddy,' 'mommy,' 'Laura,' 'more,' 'here,' 'birdie,' 'night-night,' 'poo-poo,' 'apple,' 'piggy,' 'duck,' 'hot,' and 'botty.'"*

"You should have put that on your college application."

"Mom, look what you wrote," she said, and as she read out loud, her voice wavered: "*Shows her belly-button, uses chair to get to sink, makes nice to kitty (very gentle), knows her own jacket, screams 'mine' at every provocation, loves playing 'gonna get ya', grabs Laura's things and runs if you say not to, does it to be funny, is very friendly.*"

"You always had a great sense of humor," I said, but she wasn't listening to me anymore.

"I didn't get over waking at night until 20 months," she marveled.

"After you'd give me a hug and a bottle, I'd go back to sleep easily." She began reading again: "*Talks a blue streak — 'Where's Laura?' and 'Wipe it up' after she spills her milk on purpose.*" Julie giggled. "*Listens and understands 'The Three Bears' and 'The Three Little Pigs.' Knows everyone in this family goes in the potty but her and couldn't care less.*"

I didn't interrupt.

"It says here I was pretty aggressive," Julie added. "I got very angry, but I didn't throw tantrums, and I used to get over it fairly easily."

"You used to hide under your bed and sulk, and your Dad would crawl under with you and suck his fingers until you started to laugh."

"I was very uninhibited," Julie continued. She was enjoying herself immensely by now. "I jumped into my baby pool and thought I could swim. I was mostly good-natured and reasonable. I knew pins were sharp and the stove was hot. And I was very affectionate, it says."

"You were." I remembered how cuddly she'd been.

"And very smiley," she went on quietly. "Once when you came back from shopping, I looked into your eyes and said, 'Happy.'"

She looked up at me, her eyes brimming with tears.

"What?" I asked. My own eyes were damp.

I knew something very important was happening. I could see it in the way her face softened. All these years Julie had believed that somehow her sister's arrival had seemed a bigger miracle to us than her own, that we had watched our firstborn more closely, or cared more deeply, or taken more pleasure in someone else. And now, in words it hadn't taken more than a few minutes to scribble, she'd come across evidence that her most ordinary activities had been noted with delight.

In her baby book, she'd stumbled on a different mother from the one she'd judged and found wanting. And she'd come across a different child from the one who'd always felt overshadowed by an older sister.

Who knows why people change or how rifts heal? I only know I still get tearful when I remember what I learned that afternoon.

Of all the lessons in parenting I want to share with my brother and sister-in-law, this is the one that accompanies this gift: Even when it's hidden away for eighteen years in the pages of a baby book, no love is ever wasted.

February 1988

WHEN MY DAUGHTER Laura first told me she and Brian had chosen a date for their wedding, she was disappointed that I wasn't more excited.

"Mom, this is the most important day in my life," she chided.

"Sweetheart, you know I'm delighted you're marrying Brian," I explained. "I'm just thinking about how much work a wedding's going to be."

My friend Joan had sent me two typewritten pages listing the preparations she'd made for her son's Bar Mitzvah, and I was worried about all the physical work to be done — fixing up the house, making lists, pulling all the loose ends together. I never envisioned how much *mental* energy this one day in our lives would require.

When my husband, the dog, and I are in bed, we spend the moments before sleep thinking of the perfect wedding.

"It would be nice if the dog could take part in the wedding," my husband says, scratching a furry ear.

"I don't see why Buckwheat can't come down the aisle with me before the ceremony," I say. "I think he'd look great in a bow tie, but I've already asked Laura about including the dog. She said absolutely not. In fact, the dog's not even invited to the reception. We have to board him somewhere." I wonder how the two of us ever raised a child who wants a proper wedding. Still, after all these years as parents, Jack and I are prepared to accept almost anything.

When my husband, the dog, and I go places in the car, we wile away the miles, imagining the wedding we'd have if it were up to us.

"I could learn to play the wedding march on my tuba," my husband says, foot steady on the gas.

"Oh, hon, I don't know," I say gently. The man beside me, who played trumpet as a teen-ager, bought an old battered tuba at a yard sale last summer and now considers himself the master of six songs. He's gotten a lot of attention lately for playing "When the Saints Go Marching In" with our neighborhood pick-up band on the Fourth of July, and it's unhinged his judgment. Although I haven't dared to say this out loud, I suspect the crowd's enthusiasm was for his nerve, not his talent.

"They've already hired someone to play music at the wedding," I hint.

"I know, I know," he says sadly. I sympathize. After all these years of ooohing and ahhhing over homemade pot holders and Styrofoam pictures, how could our child prefer professional to strictly amateur? Still, after a lifetime of compromise, we've come to accept her limitations.

Later, I am browsing at Building Nineteen, a local discount house, when I come across six pale lavender bridesmaid's dresses with scalloped hems and puffy sleeves. Their original price tags read $160; the going price is $29.99. They look a little like crocheted tablecloths, but they're cheap. I get Laura's permission to buy them all, then wait for her verdict when she comes home for the weekend.

"Gee, they're not the way I pictured them from your description," she says firmly. "They're nice, but not really what I want."

"Think of how much money the bridesmaids will save."

"Think about how strange they'll look in those dresses," Laura says.

I return the dresses without a word of protest, pondering the capriciousness of life. She must not have inherited my gene for getting incredible bargains if she can consider paying full price. Still, after all these years of social turmoil, nothing surprises me anymore.

Why do I always have to have limited input into weddings, including my own? As I recall, I studied for final exams while my mother hired the hall, the caterer, the florist, and musicians. All I had to do was show up. How can history be repeating itself when I'm so full of good ideas?

My husband, the dog, and I sit around the dinner table, bemoaning the guest list as it now stands. After we made up a list of relatives from both families and included all the kids' friends, there wasn't room for most of the friends we've made in the past twenty years.

"We could have a party after the kids come back from their honeymoon," I say. "The house and yard will still look terrific. We can invite everyone we know and, if we're lucky, there might be food left over from the wedding."

"It would be nice to do it the way we want it," Jack says, clinching the deal.

Snow falls outside, but indoors the sun shines. We dream of spring when I'll send out informal gray invitations with white ferns instead of the formal black-and-white ones the kids chose. We'll dress the dog in bow tie and pleated bib and treat him like a guest of honor. My husband will play "Here Comes the Bride" on his tuba and receive a deafening round of applause. And I will shamelessly wear a beautiful dress that cost an unbelievably low price.

I'm sure Laura and Brian will cooperate. It can't be any harder for them to go along with our plans than it will be for us to pretend at their wedding that we are the well-within-normal, highly con- ventional mother and father of the bride.

THERE'S ONE THING I always knew about my home-town: As soon as I could, I was getting out of it.

My feelings had nothing to do with the city of Worcester, which is where my mother and her sisters had chosen to spend their lives. It was just that, having higher ambitions for their children, they taught us that the path to success would inevitably lead us somewhere else.

I enjoyed growing up as part of a boisterous, extended family, but I was never taught to value it. I saw the arguments, the meddling, and the competition through my mother's eyes and considered all that wrangling a high price to pay. I ignored my own particular pleasures — a grandfather who encouraged me to write, cousins who valued me as a tomboy, homes where I was always welcome — and had no qualms about severing those connections when I went off to college. The older generation, who'd never had the chance to go off on their own, shoved their young out of the nest, and we left without a backward glance.

For a long time, I fully expected my own children to follow the same path. I echoed my mother and father: *Never look back. Get away while you can.* I recited by rote: *You have to cut the cord.* I wanted my daughters to be independent, and I equated that with far away. I was sad but proud when they both left for colleges in other states.

Then my daughter Laura and her husband, Brian, returned to the Boston area after six years away. They rented an apartment in Newton, close to Brian's family, then bought a house in the town adjoining ours a year later. And before our daughter Julie and her boyfriend Chris left for graduate programs in South Carolina, where his family lives, they decided to spend the summer with us.

I couldn't understand why my grown children were still around. Had my husband and I done something wrong?

I was the one with doubts. Now that my mind was centered on adult concerns, I was loathe to get dragged back into my kids' orbit. How was I going to separate myself from their problems? Given my natural exuberance, how would I keep my hands off their lives? What was wrong with them? Didn't they know me well enough to suspect I might be a problem?

"Listen," said my husband. "They love us."

I don't know why that made me cry. It was all I had wanted from the day of their birth, but I wasn't prepared. I was too aware of all the faults that could make my children prefer to love me long distance, but evidently they thought I was flexible enough to fit into their lives without driving them crazy. They'd thought it over long and hard and had concluded it would enrich their lives to be close to their parents.

Mine isn't an isolated experience. More and more of my friends' children are returning to this area to live. These kids have spent time successfully living on their own and have made the decision to return in order to stay in close contact with their families.

"I never really knew my grandparents," says one young woman, "and when my husband and I thought about having a family, we liked the idea of having some intergenerational continuity."

"We felt that our roots were here, and we wanted to be part of a stable community," says another newly married man.

"My parents are fun," says a bachelor who lives in Boston and often spends weekends with his folks. "I don't feel like a child when I'm with them. They don't put restrictions on my behavior any more. If anything, they actually enlarge my options."

I would have thought it lunacy to invite my parents and their friends to a party of mine, and yet, when Laura and Brian throw their annual Christmas party at our house, our close friends are on their guest list. I went to another intergenerational party over the holidays and spent the evening discussing politics with the sons of an old friend.

Sociologists may refer to parents as the last remaining stabilizing forces in this society, but I feel as if all these grown children are destabilizing our peaceful old age in a beneficial way. They're keeping us young and, to be frank, in our place. Gone are the days when Mom and Dad had the last word. Instead, the old lines of authority are giving way to an occasionally uncomfortable, but crucial, honesty. I soon discovered that I wasn't in danger of getting sucked into my kids' lives. Years of independence had gotten them used to making their own decisions, and it was easy to figure out when my advice was wanted and when it wasn't.

My children told me.

I think my generation took a wrong turn. We wanted to stand on our own two feet, and too often found ourselves alone and unsupported, with no one to turn to when we needed help. We couldn't imagine being adults in our parents' presence, and so our children never got to know what it meant to be a cousin or a nephew or a grandchild. We considered dependence a weakness. Our children see interdependence as a strength. We viewed family ties as chains that would limit our freedom. Now our children welcome the security an extended family offers in hard times.

This is the cycle of life ongoing.

Each generation learns from its mistakes, but some lessons are more welcome than others. This one has brought the generations together.

"YOUR DAUGHTERS MUST have gone through a rebellious stage," says a friend whose kids are just entering high school. "How did you handle it when they deliberately did things to drive you crazy?"

I didn't know how to answer her. In my experience, calling something "rebellion" usually makes it worse.

Of course in the process of growing up, my daughters did everything adolescents are expected to do in this society, including staying out past their curfew, skipping school, drinking alcohol, using fake IDs, and keeping their rooms messy. Laura got into a car with a boy who'd been smoking grass. Julie got caught shoplifting a pair of socks. They got into automobile accidents, dated boys we would never have chosen, and had parties to which the police were summoned. ("In case you get any calls, I wanted to tell you that our daughter is having a party tonight," I once told the Marblehead police. "The name's Weltner and my address is . . . " "We know where you live," the officer replied dryly.)

I'd give more examples, but these are the only ones my kids are willing to let me share.

My husband and I gave them advice. They often ignored it. We warned them of consequences. Sometimes they decided to find out for themselves. Still, we never labeled their behavior "rebellion." We considered it learning by trial-and-error, not striking out at us. When we found out about such things (from them, for the most part), we continued to hold on to our belief that they wanted to follow the values we lived by as much as we wanted them to.

We rarely punished them. Julie paid for the stolen socks by sending part of her summer's earnings to the Globe Santa, but "the ultimate punishment would have been to lose your trust," she said when I ran this column by her. Through every crisis, we tried to keep in mind that we were all on the same side.

Take the choice of a mate, an issue that causes havoc in many families. We could have considered it an act of rebellion when Laura married outside our religion. Or, considering how fervently my husband and I have opposed nuclear power, for Julie to have fallen in love with a man whose father's occupation involves nuclear weapons plants. We believed, instead, that they were following their hearts.

I admit, I may have lifted my eyes heavenward once or twice and asked, "God, is this a test?" but I knew that every action my children took was open to more than one interpretation. Is a child rejecting her parents' values, or formulating her own? Is she refusing to be what others want her to be, or following her own desires? Is he doing this to spite someone, or to please himself? Parents get to make the call.

We get to choose how we see it.

Rebellion is in many ways the more comforting choice. For all the pain and anger that go with it, rebellion still bespeaks connection. The child who reacts against a parental value system remains within its boundaries, like a bowling ball that follows the rules whether it heads straight down the lane or races wildly down the gutter. The child in rebellion pays homage to her parents' beliefs by being "bad" according to their definition.

Holding to a rigid set of beliefs that doesn't take a child's wishes and needs into account creates a situation ripe for rebellion, but real independence is a different matter. It's far more difficult to the extent that it marks a genuine separation between the parties. Used to being the center of a child's existence, parents can feel lost out there on the periphery. The moment when parents realize they are no longer their child's major point of reference is a sobering one.

I remember a call I got from Julie when she was in college. A friend had invited her south for spring vacation. She was excited, she said, though she had nothing to wear and no time to shop. I thought I'd surprise her with a new bathing suit, shorts, and a shirt. She called to thank me when they arrived in the mail, but when she came home for the summer, I found the outfit in her closet, tags still attached.

I wasn't hurt that she didn't like my taste because I hadn't used my taste. I'd gone to her favorite store and, putting myself in her place, chosen clothing I thought she would like. What hurt was that I didn't know her taste any more, that I could no longer assume I knew her well enough to put myself in her place. My "child" had become someone else.

This happens a lot to those of us with grown kids. For some reason, no one warns us that one day our children will think thoughts different from ours, and not necessarily the opposite either, but something entirely outside our repertoire. Though it's tempting to criticize or argue as a way of trying to draw our children back into our frame of reference, eventually the truth smacks us in the face. They've become adults whose thoughts we can't read, whose decisions we can't always predict, and whose choices we don't fully understand.

I wasn't prepared for this. Just a generation ago, adults didn't let on that they no longer shared what they considered their parents' prejudices. Good children, even fully-grown ones, were discreet, polite, and dishonest in their parents' company. Love meant keeping a parent's illusions intact, but times have changed. We told our children when they were small that we would love them no matter what they did. It's only logical that now they think we should love them no matter what they *think*.

Even when we're convinced we know better.

Once I loved my own reflection in my children. Now it's time to hold the unfamiliar in that same warm embrace. Once I knew my kids through and through. Now I need to turn up the love until it encompasses not only our shared values, but their misguided opinions, their ill-founded convictions, and their ridiculous ideas.

And mine.

October 1991

LAURA WENT TO RUN an errand, leaving me in the car with my granddaughter, Jessie, now seven months old. The front seat's headrest provided the perfect cover for a game of peek-a-boo. Jessie was in her car seat behind me.

By the time Laura returned, I'd succeeded in coaxing a chortle out of Jessie.

"I love playing with babies," I said. "I'm having just as much fun with Jessie as I did with you when you were her age."

"What do you mean, Mom?" Laura responded, puzzled. "I didn't know you had fun playing with me. All you ever say is how hard it was."

I stared at her as if she were crazy. I felt accused, bewildered, and angry. I wanted to silence her, to insist she take such an unfair statement back. What kind of a mother did she think I'd been? But I didn't defend myself. If I've learned anything in all these years, it's that the most helpful response to any perceived attack is a question.

"What are you talking about?" I asked.

"Well, you always say how isolated you were, and how difficult it was to make friends, and how overwhelmed you felt with Dad away so much. I didn't know you ever had fun with me."

I was silent all the way home, but that night I replayed the stories I'd told my daughters about my early experiences as a mother, trying to see what messages I might have inadvertently given Laura.

I spread them out like beads on a string: how Laura resisted breast-feeding, and how it was only my stubbornness that kept me from resorting to a bottle; how, in spite of doctors' warnings about the dangers of smothering newborns, I took her into our bed at night; how she cried for four solid hours on a train ride she and I took; how her father and I used to toss a handful of Cheerios into her playpen so that we could sleep late Saturday mornings; how Jack and I had to drive her around in the car until she fell asleep so we could talk; how our beagle once choked her with his chain; how difficult it was to make friends with other mothers when babies were always sick, napping, or interrupting us.

The context for all these stories was the fact that, when Laura was four months old, I followed Jack to an army base in New Jersey, and while he was busy round the clock running a psychiatric clinic, I was left alone to cope as best I could. In that setting, my selective memory seemed to have focused on the difficulties I'd had dealing with the demands of a new baby on my own.

I racked my brain for some unambivalent story. We have movie scenes of me playing peek-a-boo with Laura on a swing, and shots of her fearlessly jumping into my arms in a swimming pool, but there are no stories to go with them. The only positive tale I came up with was how we used to construct elaborate block buildings together, but I always used that one as an example of how sad it was that I'd had to turn my child into my best friend.

I'd ruthlessly abridged my version of Laura's childhood, letting all the joyful moments slip through my fingers like sand. I'd edited out the magic — the softness of her skin, the delicious smell of her hair, the flash of intelligence in her eyes. I'd erased the miracles — her first smile, her first step, her first word. I'd highlighted all the troubling events and overlooked the moments of pure happiness, assuming that, without my telling her, Laura would somehow know what I knew: that her presence in my life had revealed a capacity for love within me that I'd never even imagined before my children were born.

Memories are like photos in an album. Moments, caught in the flashbulb's quick flare of light, stand out against the dark background that is the ordinary routine of life. And yet, over the same period of time, one could shoot an altogether different set of pictures, showing a different succession of events, other moods, a change of emphasis, depending upon the purpose. I'd clung to stories that reflected my sense of myself as a displaced person, struggling without support in a strange place. But there was another story, equally true, about a mother who loved her child with all her heart.

This morning, I sit before my computer, tugging on another string that winds its way through Laura's earliest years, recalling events that have been waiting within me, unvoiced, for more than a quarter of a century: the thrill of holding a sticky infant in my arms immediately after delivery; the sight of Laura slipping peacefully into sleep after breast-feeding; blowing noisily into her belly button when I changed her diaper; my rush of joy when Laura stretched out her pudgy arms to be lifted; the songs her father and I made up and can still recall; the pleasure of watching her gentle ways with a doll; her face, smeared with frosting and alive with pleasure, at her first birthday party.

How could I have tucked these moments into one of my mind's closets and shut the door? How many other happy memories — from my own childhood, from the early years of our marriage — have I buried under a mountain of carefully selected predicaments? I created a consistent vision of myself, but at what cost?

"We are all storytellers, and the story that consumes us the most is the one we tell about our own lives," writes Peggy Penn, a family therapist. "There are many stories that may fit any individual's life."

I think it's time for a serious rewrite.

December 1991

WHEN OUR YOUNGER daughter, Julie, told us that she and Chris wanted to get married in July, I was supremely confident I could turn what many might consider the drudgery of planning a wedding into a grand endeavor.

After all, Jack and I had envisioned our secluded lawn, with its large trees and flowering bushes, as the perfect setting for an outdoor reception right from the beginning. We bought our house, in part, because we could picture it as the site of an elegant summer wedding, and we'd just recently had it painted. As for the ceremony, when we joined the Unitarian-Universalist Church, one of its attractions was how easily I could picture my daughters, toddlers at the time, walking down its lovely center aisle.

Laura's wedding had lavishly fulfilled all the house's promises. In my attic the twenty ceramic vases I'd used as centerpieces at her wedding were waiting to be filled with Impatiens seedlings again. In my files were the names of caterers, florists, dressmakers, photographers, musicians, rental places, and bed and breakfasts, along with gifts ideas and suitable readings for the ceremony.

I was prepared for everything, that is, except what happened.

"Chris and I don't want to have our reception in the yard," Julie said to me so matter-of-factly that I didn't believe her.

"Of course you do," I countered. "Everything will be blooming then."

"Mom," Julie said quietly, "This is our wedding, and we don't want our guests to be eaten alive by insects. We want the reception indoors."

I bit my tongue and dropped the subject. Twenty-four hours later Julie informed me that she and Chris didn't want to be married in our church, either. "It gets so hot there in the summer," she insisted. "If we have a heat wave, I'll sweat to death."

I felt the urge to argue, but I controlled myself.

Until I was alone with my husband.

"Everything I want, she wants the opposite," I muttered to him through clenched teeth. "I'm trying my best to make the planning as enjoyable as the wedding itself, but there's no pleasing that child. She's impossible." I was uncomfortably aware that I was in the process of turning the person I was supposed to be cooperating with into the enemy.

"She doesn't want Laura's wedding," my husband said, and

suddenly all the pieces fell into place. Of course. No wonder she didn't want to see the words from Laura's ceremony, or hire a DJ, or have the rehearsal dinner in Marblehead. I'd been thinking along family lines, feeling an at-home wedding was "our" way of marrying, while Julie viewed the last wedding as a reflection of Laura's personality. She wanted something uniquely her own.

I could support that with a whole heart.

Julie and I got into another "disagreement" during our family vacation in South Carolina. We were all leaving for the airport and, trying to be efficient, I announced that Julie and Chris should return our keys to the rental office before joining the rest of us at a restaurant for breakfast. When they'd completed the task I'd assigned, Julie summoned me outside for a private talk.

"Mom, I would have appreciated it if you'd *asked* us to return the key instead of volunteering us," she said, with a great deal of feeling. "You do that all the time. It's as if my wishes don't matter to you at all."

"I'm sorry," I said, hiding how annoyed I was. How could her father and I have raised a child who wasn't willing to do her parents a favor? How could she feel that helping us out was an imposition? My apology really meant, "I regret having asked you to do anything, you rotten kid," but what kept me from flying into a rage was that somewhere deep inside me I'm aware that I construct these monsters who live in my kids' skins. I don't know where they come from, but I do know enough to check them out. On the flight home, I asked Laura for a second opinion.

"Mom, Julie's on her own now and proud of her independence. Then you come along and treat her like an extension of yourself, as if she isn't a separate person whose wishes need to be taken into account," Laura explained. "It's how you asked that bothered her, not having to take the key back."

Now Julie's behavior made sense to me.

I used to hide my annoyance at my mother when we were together, but it didn't bring us any closer. It gave me migraine headaches and left us both feeling distant and estranged, especially since I then got to take all that negativity home and keep it. I've encouraged my children to be honest with me (though, the Lord knows, I'm not always happy to have my faults pointed out) because I'm convinced that the only way people actually let go of critical feelings is by expressing them.

Then it's my job to listen, to decide how valid their criticisms are, and choose whether to change or not, without tripping on my own hurt feelings.

This time I asked Julie to coach me by pointing out each time I requisitioned her services without asking. A week later, we talked on the phone until we felt right again, a flawed mother and her imperfect, but well-meaning, child.

Like everyone else, I'd like to be perfect. It's difficult to give up the wish to some day rise above everybody else's criticism. I grew up with parents who thought their job was to correct me, though I was supposed to hold my tongue. Then I encouraged my daughters to speak their minds while I concentrated on giving positive feedback.

I can feel like the filling in a generational sandwich, squashed my whole life from above and below. Or I can feel incredibly lucky to be growing more and more comfortable with the truth.

I don't want to end up someplace perfect.

I'm trying to get someplace real.

July 1993

I RARELY TRAVEL without my husband, so when I traveled solo to Columbia, South Carolina, where my younger daughter and her husband now live, I was delighted to find Julie waiting for me at the gate. When Julie and Chris brought me back to the airport three days later, I was surprised at how different this visit had been from all the others.

Instead of interacting with my husband, I had the chance to observe my daughter's world and the time to reflect. I gained a new appreciation for her relationship with Chris and concluded that if the love the two of them lavish upon my grandkittens and my tropical grandfish is any indication, they'll make wonderful parents.

I also figured out why Julie no longer resembles the teen-ager I thought needed so much improving.

When she was a teen-ager, I hassled her daily because her room was always a wreck. She didn't know how to clean it. I'd go into a room she'd supposedly straightened and find that she'd stuffed piles of paper in her drawers or hung wrinkled clothing in her closet. I blamed myself for not being more like Martha Stewart. After all, Julie had learned to drop things on the floor by observing me. I worried no one would be able to live with her. Like a crazed fortune teller, I saw outraged roommates and a furious husband in her future.

Julie's eating habits were another source of friction. Every bite of junk food was a red flag in my face. I tried to hold my tongue, terrified that my nagging would create an eating disorder, but I couldn't help pointing out certain nutritional facts — the amount of fat in a Big Mac, the benefits of vegetables, a woman's need for calcium — again and again and again.

Julie and I had this little dance going, a regimented push and pull that got us nowhere. I prodded; she resisted. I suggested; she ignored. Every morning I vowed not to criticize. Every evening, I regretted having put my foot in my mouth again. One moment I held myself responsible for the tension between us; the next I blamed her. We couldn't seem to get through a single day without conflict.

I went to see a mentor at the Option Institute, determined to figure out why I couldn't disentangle myself from this fruitless struggle. I suspected it was because what bothered me most about my own mother was that she was messy and overweight. As a child, I was so embarrassed by the clutter in our house that I never invited friends over. I also worried about my mother's health, especially her diabetes, but no matter how much I criticized her eating habits, she continued to indulge her love of sweets. I hated having so little impact on her behavior. I hated not being able to change her. Now here I was again, a grown woman, experiencing helplessness around the same issues I thought I'd put behind me forever.

"My daughter is my mother all over again," I explained to the mentor. "I can't bear having to live through this again."

"Julie may be similar to your mom in some regards, but why do you say she's just like her?" he asked.

I stopped, bewildered by the question. Then an entirely new perspective clicked into place.

"I see what you mean," I said, trying to slip my daughter out from under her grandmother's shadow. In fact, Julie was very different from my mother in personality, in interests, even in body type and energy level. By the end of the hour, I couldn't imagine how I'd ever confused them.

I never mentioned this session to Julie. I didn't think she'd appreciate my talking about her to a stranger, but I no longer winced when she ate ice cream or shuddered when I peeked into her room. I didn't notice a change in Julie's habits, but she no longer had to be different for me to be comfortable. Things simply quieted down between us.

That first night I arrived in Columbia, my son-in-law made dinner, a delicious cauliflower-and-tomato casserole without a drop of fat. The next night Julie baked chicken without the skin. There were apples in the refrigerator for snacks. She cleaned up as she cooked. We each washed our dishes when dinner was over. She made the bed in the morning and put the mail away after looking through it, two things I never do. There were moments I thought I was visiting some other woman's child.

This is how I understand what happened: My fault-finding trapped Julie in a defensive posture, locking her into the very behaviors I was trying to extinguish. Once I let go of my judgments, Julie no longer had to put all her energy into fighting me, which gave her the freedom to think about what she wanted for herself. And these trivial issues, which I'd blown out of proportion because of my own history, eventually ceased to be a problem for either of us.

That's not Julie's version, but what does she know?

She thinks she just grew up.

A FRIEND TOLD ME this story: His mother was sent home from the hospital with cancer, fully aware that she was going to die. She loved having her family fuss over her, but more than anything else she wanted to say good-bye to her best friend, Evelyn.

My friend called Evelyn's home and left the message, "Mother would love to see you." His call was not returned. The next day he reached the woman's husband, who said his wife was at a meeting. He promised she'd call back, but she didn't. Urgent phone calls to Evelyn began to alternate with the lame excuses my friend made up to tell his mom.

"Evelyn's not feeling well herself," my friend fibbed to his mother. "She had to visit her daughter," he lied. "She'll come just as soon as she can." On the day his mother lay dying, surrounded by her husband and children, her eyes filled with tears. "Where's Evelyn?" she asked.

This time, her question met with anguished silence.

The funeral was well attended. Many of her friends, including Evelyn, showed up to pay their respects. "I loved your mother so much I couldn't bear to see her suffer," she whispered to my friend, expecting sympathy. He turned away before she could see the fury in his eyes.

"What did she mean by love?" he asked me, weeks later. "If you avoid someone who needs you, is that love? If you're thinking of your feelings and not of hers, is that love? What good is love if you don't back it up? What is love good for if you don't make it tangible?"

I had no answers for him, but in spite of my sympathy for his mother, I understood Evelyn's behavior. It reminded me of a time when I thought loving someone meant you took on their suffering as your own, when I believed caring meant feeling another's pain, even if it disabled you.

As a result, at a crucial point in my life, I abandoned my older daughter when she desperately needed me.

Right before her high-school graduation, Laura slipped a disc in her back. I felt more helpless and anxious than I had when my own disc had ruptured years before. At the end of a summer of bed rest, when she went off to college in a full body brace, I accompanied her in spirit. I stretched out on imaginary classroom floors to take exams. I felt as if I lay sleepless in her dorm room, imprisoned in an uncomfortable plastic corset. I merged with her in my mind, but I was unavailable in real life. Whenever my daughter called home, I handed the phone to my husband.

I loved her so much, I couldn't bear to deal with what was happening to her. I was so upset, I couldn't trust myself to hide how I was feeling. I was so frightened about what her future might hold, I feared my voice would betray me. I felt tremendously concerned, but what good did that do anyone? When she needed me, I wasn't there.

It wasn't until my friend spoke about "making love tangible" that I was able to look beyond my own feelings. I'd thought falling into a pit of despair and dread was a sign of my love, when it actually made it impossible for me to be comfortable with my daughter's suffering. I didn't see that when people are in difficult situations we can't fix, making love tangible requires being able to respond from a peaceful inner place. After all, the last thing someone in trouble needs is to end up having to comfort the person to whom they've turned for support.

How can you stay peaceful when someone, or God forbid, everyone, you love is falling apart? In my case, I had to seriously address these questions: What attitude would allow me to remain present without feeling too anxious? What inner response could keep me from feeling overwhelmed? When I finally saw how my absorption of my daughter's fear and sadness had kept me from meeting her needs, I realized how important it was for me to maintain my own emotional equilibrium, no matter what was happening around me.

Sometimes it still feels odd to make a conscious choice not to take on a child's unhappiness. It's taken practice to see myself as a separate person who allows others to experience the intensity of their own emotions all by themselves. Still, I've learned it's a choice I can make because, by honoring the boundaries between us, I see myself becoming more constant, competent, and caring.

Laura knows how deeply I regret having let her down, and this is how I apologized: I learned to say "I love you" by being there.

June 1996 IN TWO WEEKS my husband, Jack, and I fly south to help our younger daughter, Julie, and Chris pack up their belongings. Then the four of us will drive two cars and a U-Haul truck back to Massachusetts. The kids and their two cats will be living with us until Julie and Chris find jobs and figure out where they want to live.

I can't believe how excited I am at the prospect.

Oh, I know the old saying, "Life begins when your youngest child goes off to college and the dog dies," but when Julie left for college and Buckwheat died, we got another dog.

Our friends were puzzled by Pandora's appearance. Having survived parenthood, they couldn't understand why we'd want another living soul dependent on us for everything. Why would we choose to go through the hassle of training a puppy? Why limit our freedom by having to arrange our schedules around a dog's needs, never mind having to get dog-sitters when we went on vacation? After all, the argument went, we'd devoted two decades of our life to raising our children. Hadn't we earned a well-deserved rest from all these responsibilities?

Know what?

Resting is vastly overrated.

It's been six years since our older daughter, Laura, and Brian came to live in the next town, allowing us to play an active part in helping them raise their children. We spend time each week with our grandkids, Jessie and Danny, but not from a sense of obligation. We feel we have a valuable contribution to make. We don't feel put-upon when we're asked to help out on special occasions, either. In fact, the time I spend with my grandchildren is the most spontaneous, fun-filled part of my week. Often, when I'm on my own, I find myself wishing I had them with me.

I'm hopeless. I enjoy caring for the people I love. Mothering is the thing I do best. Why would I ever reject the most satisfactory aspect of myself?

I guess I'm not a woman of the nineties, striding forward to bigger and supposedly better things. This stage of my life is supposed to be mine to do as I please, without taking anyone else's wishes into consideration. I could be marketing myself more aggressively as a public speaker, mastering the Internet, or searching for a condo that would require less care than this big old house of ours. Instead, I've planted a giant pumpkin vine that requires almost as much attention as another child.

If I made a list of priorities with my brain, sewing matching taffeta holiday dresses for Jessie and her doll would never make the list. Nor would building Danny a two-story castle from Styrofoam packing material, though that's how I spent three hours last weekend. I can't convince anyone, least of all myself, that such projects have any part to play in furthering my career, advancing the causes of civilization, or bringing about world peace.

But if I make a list of priorities with my heart, I have no problem deciding what to do. I feel happy when I'm useful. I love feeling that I have a role to play in my children's lives, though it requires a very different set of skills now that they're grown. I take it as a great compliment that Julie and Chris would even consider spending time under our roof after six years on their own. We'll all have to give up and give in to some degree to make this work, but the challenge of it excites me in a way few other undertakings do.

Accommodating one another won't always be comfortable, I know, but comfort isn't my highest value. Nor is the ability to keep on doing things the way I've always done them. I don't have to have everything in this house my own way to feel empowered. I want to keep stretching and growing until I die, and believe me, there's nothing that keeps you stretching and growing like children in close proximity.

OK, now I'll rest.

My case.

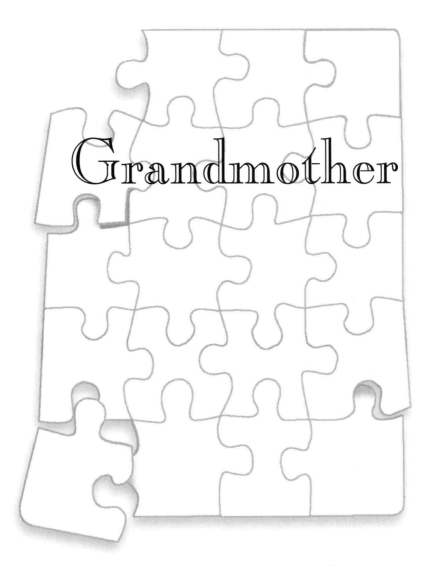

Grandmother

I FOUND A BABY'S CRADLE

January 1991

at a yard sale last summer. It sat by a picket fence, its walnut stain badly scratched, and it squeaked every time it rocked. Still, the price was right, and the three lively children helping their mom sell their outgrown belongings testified to its nurturing powers. I brought it home and tucked it away.

Last week, with about a month before my first grandchild's due date, I began the happy task of transformation.

While I sanded, I listened to Congress debate whether our country should go to war in the Persian Gulf. As I spread three coats of white paint over the slatted sides, the minutes leading up to the U.N. deadline slowly ran out. I was sewing yellow fabric over cradle bumpers when the first reports of victory in the air appeared on TV screens all over the world. And as I sewed a mattress cover, word came that rockets had been launched over Tel Aviv.

Back in the sixties, when the threat of nuclear war hung like a shadow over every undertaking, friends often gave "How can anyone choose to bring a child into this world?" as their reason not to have children. With two small children clinging to my skirts, what could I say? That I believed that nothing could ever take away the years a family has together? That I hoped no amount of suffering could nullify the moments of happiness we might have? That, to me, loving and being loved had a value that was absolute, irrevocable, and priceless, no matter what the future might bring?

Now, twenty-five years later, that question is back, stirred up by predictions of serious ecological consequences if Saddam Hussein goes through with his threat to blow up all of Kuwait's oil wells. In this fearful climate, I sealed blue and yellow painted flowers under a coat of polyurethane and thought of the child soon to be born into this uncertain world. I'd seen the fetus in an Ultrasound close-up hours earlier — a being, eight months in utero, calmly smiling from the shadows of another world straight into the future.

Something our minister said after my mother's death came to mind: Life is like a bird that flies from the mysterious darkness outside through a window into a lighted room, stays for a short while, then flies out another window back into a darkness so profound we cannot penetrate it. I had been comforted then by the thought of my mother's life force continuing on its purposeful journey. But now, peering in the other direction, I felt as if I had been given a glimpse into the darkness beyond the window of birth. Caught by the gleam in those shining black eyes, I'd come face to face with life before life.

Tired of war news, I turned my radio dial to an FM station playing a selection of peace songs from the sixties. I put down my brush and took a step back to admire the finished product that glowed in the sunlight streaming in the window. Perhaps it was my imagination, but the cradle, silently waiting for its occupant, seemed encircled by radiance.

A child moves toward the moment of its birth, but those who await the child also move in their hearts toward that fateful meeting, as if a connection between the two has somehow already been formed in the depths of their being. At that moment, it seemed to me that my longing had become palpable, as if the deep powers from which we draw our existence were trembling before me in the air.

How can humans speak of reverence for life and, at the same time, pursue death with such a passion? We are mired in the quarrels of nations, distracting ourselves from the question that looms larger with every dollar spent waging war, not only against the enemy but upon the earth itself: *How long before we damage this planet so severely that it can no longer care for us?* Perhaps each birth is an attempt by the process that sustains life to remind us of the wastefulness of destruction.

"The same stream of life that runs through my veins night and day runs through the world and dances in rhythmic measure," wrote the Indian philosopher Rabindranath Tagore. "Is it beyond thee to be glad with the gladness of this rhythm? to be tossed and lost and broken in the whirl of this fearful joy?"

I know every new parent's eagerness is laced with fear. In every family, anticipation mingles with apprehension as the minutes leading up to a child's appearance run out, one by one. As I stood in the hall admiring my handiwork, a song playing on the radio pierced my reverie. A sweet female voice was singing about becoming a cradle in which to rock a weary world, declaring that she would sing her lullaby above the noise and pain of war. I wasn't the first, nor would I be the last woman to welcome a child into a world at war.

And so I let the music catch and comfort me in the whirl of a fearful joy.

April 1991 ALMOST EVERY WEEKDAY morning I play with my grand-daughter, Jessie, now six weeks old, while my daughter showers. When Laura settles into a rocking chair to nurse the baby, I run a load of laundry, unpack the dishwasher her husband ran the night before, and make the bed. Sometimes I baby-sit while Laura keeps an appointment or I hold the baby while she makes phone calls. By noon, I'm usually home.

Jessie has another grandmother, Anne, who browses through thrift shops for baby clothes and never visits without bringing a bag of treasures. One night a week after work, Anne and her husband come out from Newton to cook dinner in return for a chance to cuddle the baby.

I watch my daughter raising her child in a place where she has friends, and good neighbors, and a strong support network, and I see how hard a time she's still having. Like many new mothers more than a month after the baby's birth, she's not herself yet. She needs all the help she can get.

"Do you know how lucky you are to have us all?" I asked her.

"It's not luck," Laura replied. "Brian and I settled close to our families and friends on purpose."

She must have been listening carefully to the stories I've told: about how difficult it was to follow my husband into the army when she was four months old, and how I found myself in a rented house off base in New Jersey, home full-time, without a friend in the world. I thought those days were ancient history, but holding my grandchild, and feeling the unalloyed joy of her small body curled

170

against mine, brings those memories back with a vengeance.

Suddenly, I remember all too well feeling overwhelmed and lonely and tearful day after day. My parents lived far away. My husband was on duty every other night and weekends. I felt incapable of making friends. Whenever I arranged to visit another mother, one of the babies invariably took a nap or got sick. I had no one to turn to, no one who understood what I was going through. I didn't know the area or what resources might be available to a young mother.

I didn't even know I needed them.

This, I think, is the saddest part of the story: I thought I should be able to handle everything myself. I'd done well at college. I'd held down a demanding job. Surely, I could master caring for an infant. My husband agreed with me completely. I should be functioning perfectly.

I watched soap operas. A lot. I took the baby to the mall, or anywhere there were people, just to have somewhere to go. I took an adult education class but didn't connect with another soul. I made an infant my best friend and watched her absorb my anxiety. I was so desperate for my husband's company, and so enraged by his absence, that my ambivalence kept us at a painful distance. I didn't realize I was suffering the effects of isolation.

I thought I was going crazy.

One day Laura cried for hours. Nothing I did made any difference. Finally, I dressed her warmly, put her in the carriage, and rolled her out to the curb next to the garbage. Then I sat inside the house, watching and crying. To this day I don't understand my state of mind, but here it is nonetheless: I sincerely believed the garbage collectors would take her away with the trash. At the last minute, when the truck turned the corner, I dashed out and saved her, filled with horror at what I'd been thinking. That night, when my husband rose from the dinner table to spend the next twenty-four hours on duty at the hospital, I climbed into the coat closet and refused to come out.

I couldn't put into words what I needed, but I accepted my husband's evaluation of the situation. He decided that I needed help and arranged for us to see a therapist together once a week.

The therapist wasn't very skillful, but the treatment worked. I had my husband's companionship one afternoon a week, a trip to New York City to look forward to, and a chance to talk about the stress I was under. From that point on, I began the climb back to my normal neurotic self.

It took me a long time to view that young girl with compassion. Surrounded by people all her life, she'd been torn away from every support she'd come to depend on. She foolishly thought she could give unstintingly to a needy child without having any source of renewal herself. In retrospect, it's a wonder she stayed as sane as she did.

We seem to understand now that mothers were never meant to raise their children in isolation, that it isn't shameful or immature or crazy to need more support during the fourth trimester, the three-month period following birth when a mother's heightened physical and emotional vulnerability increases her need for rest and recuperation, companionship, encouragement, and reassurance.

My presence in my daughter's home isn't a luxury, it's a simple fact of life.

Mothers need mothering, too.

August 1991

I'M STRETCHED ACROSS my daughter's bed, feeding my grandchild. Jessie contentedly sucks away at the bottle I'm holding for her. At four months, she doesn't know much about the world, but her eyes, wide and unblinking, are locked onto mine. When Jessie sleeps, I see her dad in the shape of her face and the color of her skin, but when she opens her eyes and stares into mine, I feel as if I am looking past the blue-gray irises and large dark pupils all the way down to what Emerson called the Oversoul, "that within which every man's particular being is contained and made one with all other."

It isn't recognition I see there; Jessie hasn't placed me on her map yet, but there's contact and a merging of consciousness. I feel as if I could hang laundry on the beam of light that links the two of us together. From these depths, Jessie radiates curiosity, intelligence, and what seems to be an unconditional love for everything within her view. And I gaze back, empty of everything but the sight and delight of her.

With Jessie, I'm in the present, my mind uncluttered by thoughts of past or future. A voice within whispers, "*Now*," riveting my attention to this child, this interaction, this magical moment, as if the concept of time had never been discovered. For these few hours, I have no chores, no errands, no calls to return.

I am "baby-sitting" — a word that gives no clues to its magic.

It is the wondrous gift of begin-again.

What I know of my own early years is my mother's version: I was never young. I was a worry-wart, old before my time. I prefer to think of it this way: I never had confidence in the way my parents were running our family. It's only in retrospect that I see the reasons I became such a playful mother, taking more pleasure from my children's world than in the domain of adults.

Motherhood gave me my first chance to be truly young.

Until I gave my daughters a bath, I never knew how much fun it could be to soap a tummy or admire shampoo curls in a bathroom mirror. The squeals of surprise in a game of peek-a-boo were echoed in my own heart. Little piggy running "wee! wee! wee! all the way home" tickled my fancy. When I popped a baby's sticky fingers into my mouth, or had a child hold on tightly when we went swimming, I was meeting my own needs for physical affection. I took every chance I could to give myself the spontaneity and silliness I'd missed.

Just the same, as a parent it's difficult not to keep one eye on the desired outcome. I was lucky to have a best friend who shared my belief that hanging out with your children was a defensible use of a woman's time. Still Lynn and I couldn't help but feel the weight of our responsibilities as mothers. We dutifully tried to make everything we did with our children worthwhile. Our kids may have enjoyed exploring local tide pools with us, but they emerged from the experience smarter as well as wetter. We were conscious that we were shaping character, or teaching concepts, or preparing our kids to be competent adults. We often looked at our children through the eyes of a teacher, say, or a future boss, and kept in mind the way the culture might measure our success.

Now, like an undeserved blessing, here comes another chance. Gone are the ingredients that made mothering so difficult — the long hours, the isolation, the fear of not doing the right thing. Gone is the exhaustion, the discipline, the panic of enforced confinement. Jessie's mom and dad can worry about how she turns out. As a grandmother, I can put my trust in what Emerson would call Jessie's "wise silence." There is nothing I *have* to teach her. I can measure her by what Emerson calls "the soul's scale," ignoring the judgment of ordinary folks who cannot see her for the miracle she is.

My job is simple: to enjoy the pressure of Jessie' grip as she wraps her fingers around mine, to inhale the sweet smell of her, to share her perfect happiness when she has drunk her fill of milk and grandma's face. As her eyelids flutter down, I settle into a peaceful place I could never find on my own.

This bond that binds the generations is a sacred one. What I loved in my daughters, I love again in this small, trusting soul. The love that my husband and I gave to our daughters has gathered strength, traveling through them like a stream whose source and ultimate destination are forever hidden. In this moment, love becomes a tangible force as wide as an ocean, as varied as each of us is from one another.

"Jessie," I whisper, "welcome to my life. There is no greater pleasure I will ever know than to love you without expectation, without condition, and without restraint."

February 1992

THURSDAY NIGHT, 7:58 P.M. I'm standing quietly in the darkened hallway outside the room where my eleven-month-old granddaughter is supposed to be falling asleep. Jessie indicated her exhaustion by indulging in what we call serious "eye rubby," but nonetheless, she's continuing to insist loudly that she should be downstairs playing with her grandfather. It's hard listening to her cry.

When Jessie's mother, Laura, was this age, I couldn't bear it. I didn't want my child to feel alone and abandoned at bedtime, and so her father and I lingered by her bed when she cried, singing lullabies in hopes of bringing her comfort. In consequence, our bedtime visits stretched to a half hour by the time Laura was eighteen months old. By the time she was two, my husband and I felt as if we were spending our evenings chained to her bed. We finally solved the problem by letting Laura stay up with us until she dropped in her tracks.

We thought we were being caring parents, but in retrospect I can see that we amplified Laura's crying with our near-panic response. As she got older, how could she help but notice that crying made us rush to her side in a way a simple request for help didn't? We discovered further along the road that we had unwittingly taught Laura that being unhappy was an effective way to move others. It was something I believed myself then.

It's a lesson we've both had to unlearn.

Now Laura's teaching Jessie a more direct way to get what she wants. I'm amazed at how quickly Jessie masters the word "ump!" for "pick me up," and "boh-boh" for bottle. When Jessie cries for either reason, Laura calmly encourages her to put her wants into words. Laura's pointed out that my typical response to tears — "Oh, oh, the baby's crying! Is she unhappy? Can I get her something?" — signals to Jessie that she's really got something to cry about. These days, Laura reminds me to respond to Jessie's crying with unruffled calm.

And I appreciate her coaching.

This whole interaction between Laura and me feels right. When I was raising my family, I believed grandmothers were supposed to spoil their grandkids. I kept silent when my mother arrived with bags of candy, which I didn't allow in our house. I hated having to take the stuff away after she left, and I resented her for making me the "heavy." My mother, I suppose, felt that indulging my children ensured her a warm place in their hearts — but what about mine? I minded and felt guilty about minding. Though I occasionally hinted at my displeasure, I don't think my mother ever quite understood why I scowled at her so often. I see now I did us both a disservice. I was never straightforward enough for my mother to take my feelings seriously.

I aim to be a different kind of grandmother. I live too close to my daughter to upset her equilibrium with every visit. I remind myself that since Laura knows my views on parenting, there's no need to keep repeating them. Instead, I need to learn how to support her and Brian.

I don't remember ever being told that children had a lot to teach their parents, but in a magazine called the *Family Therapy Networker*, I came across this wonderful quote in a movie review by Frank Pittman: "The mother-daughter relationship in 'Terms of Endearment' is wonderful because it is reciprocal. Like all successful parents, the mother has raised a child who knows her parents' fears and prejudices and inhibitions, and who goes forth to test and overcome those limitations . . . As with all successful parent-child relationships, once the child is comfortable with the world, she can return to raise the parents, to help them through the changes she has learned to negotiate. It is a lifelong reciprocity, unequal only at the beginning and the end."

"Lifelong reciprocity." What a wonderful phrase.

No more responsibility to be Ms. Infallible, Grandma Know-It-All. No more need to have definitive answers or the ultimate correct advice. I'm free to change. I don't have to do what I've always done any longer. I'm free to fit into my daughters' and grandchildren's lives. This is the reward that comes when you remain in relationship with your grown-up children: You get to take part in life's continuing education.

For example, take this allowing-Jessie-to-cry-a-bit-at-bedtime technique. I'm trying it out on an experimental basis. I'm leery of this theory that babies can learn to comfort themselves . . . It doesn't feel right to think of crying as a way of discharging irritability . . . I'm certainly not going to stand passively by if Jessie's plaintive cries escalate into sobbing . . .

Oops, she's asleep. Time: 8:05 P.M.

MY DAUGHTER CALLED the other day before picking up Jessie.

"Don't rush," I said cheerfully. "We're lighting matches."

There was a moment's silence, then a thoughtful, "I'll be there soon."

My daughter and her husband are trying to civilize my two-year-old granddaughter. They're teaching Jessie to brush her teeth, pick up her toys, and restrain her impulse to bite. They want her to keep her food on her plate, the pages in her books, and her shoes on her feet.

It's hard to parent a child these days, and my natural inclinations aren't making it any easier for Laura and Brian. They're often taken aback at my style of baby-sitting.

They retrieve a child who's covered her chin with lipstick, smeared her cheeks with rouge, and streaked her forehead with eye shadow. The one time Laura turned to me for an explanation, I looked like a clown myself. Jessie had spent a good half hour decorating my face with the contents of my make-up bag.

When I took Jessie to feed the ducks at a golf course, a multitude of geese appeared, determined to get at our load of bread one way or another. With Jessie on my shoulders, I had to fight my way back to the car through a cackling horde of determined water fowl. The first time, we were taken aback. Now it's our idea of an excellent adventure. During a big storm last fall, I took Jessie to a neighbor's porch to watch enormous waves pounding against the rocks below. Huddled against the door high above them, we were in no danger of getting swept away, but we did get drenched. By the time I got Jessie home to her mom, her diapers were wet from the outside.

I like to let Jessie's imagination run wild, though we gave up painting with food coloring after it got under her nails and ruined her clothing. We mix acrylic paints in ice cube trays and decorate my white dinner plates, washing them clean before the paint dries. We put bandages on vitamin bottles, counter tops and, yes, even in books. The last time Jessie took a bath at our house, she used one of her rubber frogs as a squirt gun and, aiming at our dog, Pandy, soaked the floor.

Pandy and I didn't mind a bit.

I have a high tolerance for disorder, especially since I get the house back after Jessie leaves. This is a luxury reserved for grandmas.

It's hard to explain my behavior. I'm not trying to encourage Jessie to be "naughty," though I'm aware it sometimes looks that way to my daughter. It's just that I sometimes feel so in tune with Jessie's wishes and impulses, and so childlike myself, that I can't think of a reason not to want what she wants as much as she does.

Take the matches.

Jessie had such a wonderful birthday that she invented a new name for cakes: "Happy to Yous." The words "hot," "candus," and "matchuz" immediately entered her vocabulary.

It was her idea that I light the book of matches she found on the kitchen counter. She wanted to look at the flame, to move as close to it as she dared. Looking earnestly into my eyes, she wagged her finger under my nose as she warned, "No touch, hot," before blowing each tiny fire into a spidery wisp of smoke. I entered into her concentration. I saw her evaluate the danger. And I shared Jessie's total satisfaction when our book of matches — and our interest — burned themselves out at the same time.

How can I explain? It takes a bonfire to impress me, but under Jessie's gaze, a tiny cardboard stick bursting into flame was magic. In her single-minded intensity, I came alive. If I'd been all prudence and no play, I'd have missed an unforgettable experience.

I support most of the guidelines Jessie's parents have set for her. She goes to bed on time, has a minimum of sweets at my house, and knows that whenever she cries here as well as at home, someone will say, "Put it into words," before responding. I set limits so that Jessie knows "no" means "no," wherever she is. It's just that I keep remembering what my supervisor taught me the year I was aquatic director at a summer camp:

"Before you say 'no,' always think, can I possibly say 'yes'?" she suggested. "We want these kids to have a wonderful time."

That's my philosophy of grandmothering in a nutshell.

As a mother, Laura fosters Jessie's self-control. A generation away, I encourage her spontaneity — but not unselfishly. In

Jessie's company, I'm blessed to discover within myself an inexhaustible source of laughter, my lost innocence, a delight in — OK, I'll say it — mischief.

An irresistible sprite keeps showing up inside me, wanting to play. As a grandmother, I can't help looking mature, but I've discovered an unexpected benefit at this stage of my life.

I get a second childhood.

August 1993

"I DON'T KNOW WHETHER I should go back to work full-time or not," I overheard a new mother say. "I want a career, but I don't want to miss my baby's first step or her first word."

Her comment made sense at the time, but in thinking it over, I've come to the conclusion that being there for all those "firsts" is not what makes a difference. Even if I wasn't there at the crucial moment, the first word my grandchild spoke to me, the first step she took in my presence were as thrilling as they could possibly be. In choosing how much time to devote to child care, the parent's losses are a minor part of the story.

It's what the child experiences that's important.

Today's mothers tend to view a young child's needs as mostly custodial. If she's fed, changed, and comforted when she cries, it's hard to imagine that tiny lump caring who does the work. The kid can't talk, doesn't complain, and, it seems, won't even remember what happened in the first few years of her life. Why should it matter if you hand over this tedious, menial job to someone else?

That's a hard concept to challenge when few parents feel they have options. So many single mothers with little choice in the matter. So many working mothers and fathers trying to make ends meet. So many parents whose careers are an essential aspect of their identity. Yet I think many parents would choose to spend more time at home if they understood the full impact of their absence.

While reading Amitai Etzioni's provocative book *The Spirit of*

Community: Rights, Responsibilities, and the Communitarian Agenda, I came to a full stop at the following sentence: "If all that children receive is custodial care and morally careless education, their bodies will mature but their souls will not." I felt the impact of that statement because I can see two-year-old Jessie's soul emerging like a freight train rushing at full speed from a dark tunnel. I feel, these days, as if I am catching glimpses into the inner mystery of her being.

Excited to see me after a week's separation, Jessie buried her head in my chest, then turned, and bit my arm. I yelped, then heard her whisper her mother's words to herself, "Gentle, gentle," as she tenderly stroked the tooth marks away. Taking a cookie from me on the Fourth of July, she made her way to her cousin Sarah's side, murmuring, "Let's do sharin.' " Struggling to open a tube of water-colors, she held it out to me, then changed her mind. "I do it," she insisted, and she did.

This is a child who is struggling to subdue the primitive passions inside even the most placid child, who is learning to overcome selfishness, who is growing confident of her own ability to master the obstacles in her way. She and I have been throwing elaborate parties lately, making two cupcakes, frosting them, adding sprinkles, lighting candles, singing "Happy Birthday," and, only then, eating our gorgeous concoctions. As we go about our tasks, side by side, I see Jessie's soul developing patience. She is beginning to understand that sometimes the payoff is worth the preparation.

At two, Jessie's personality is defined. Her attitude toward life is already discernible. Though she isn't consciously aware of it, she's already figured out the answers to the following questions: *How do I get what I want? Am I good or bad? Are people trustworthy? Am I competent? Am I lovable? Is there enough to go around? How can I attract people to me? Why happens when I make a mistake? Are my feelings important? Do other people bring me happiness or pain?*

There will be revisions, elaborations, and corrections as the years go on, but I can see her character forming, shaped by the values Jessie has absorbed from all of us in this short period of time. Surely, no one would disagree that providing the solid foundation every child needs is one of the most important tasks on this planet.

This is not to say children need a parent's constant, unwavering attention. My own experience as an isolated mother on an army base in New Jersey convinced me that I sorely lacked the temperament to cater to a child's needs all day long. The best companion for any child is someone who is enjoying being with her, and a mother or father can be that person for only limited periods of time. Nonetheless, the time parents spend one-on-one with a child, sharing values and encouraging the emergence of those traits that make us civilized, is more than a luxury item in a busy life. Etzioni's reexamination of parental responsibility suggests that parents and hired caregivers are not interchangeable, that children need long stretches of time with the most important people in their lives.

To thrive, children, who seem ordinary to a stranger, need the affirmation of those who see before them not only a mind and a body to cherish, but also a soul miraculously unfolding.

March 1995

PICTURE THIS: It's Monday afternoon, but instead of being alone with my four-year-old granddaughter, taking her out for lunch and to gymnastics as I do every week, I have my eleven-month-old grandson, Danny, with me as well. Laura is on a week's vacation, and I've agreed to take both children during the times neither my son-in-law nor baby-sitters are available.

It's snowing out. Luckily Jessie, Danny, and I have only one block to negotiate between the restaurant where we've just had lunch and the YMCA where we're headed for Jessie's gymnastics class. I've packed Danny back up in his snowsuit. Jessie is swaddled in her jacket, hat, scarf, and mittens. I hang my sizable pocketbook around my neck. Then I sling Danny's diaper bag over one shoulder and Jessie's backpack over the other. With my left hand I grasp the bag of toys I'm bringing to keep the baby occupied during Jessie's class. With the right, I clutch Danny and scoot him up against my body. I shuffle to the door, like some overloaded pack horse, and push.

So far, so good. We're all outdoors at least, but there's ice underfoot, and Jessie slips and falls. I stick out a foot.

"Grab my coat, hon," I say. "You can pull yourself up." I brace myself, and she gets back up on her feet. "OK, let's go." I step down from the sidewalk and look both ways, but Jessie's hanging back.

"C'mon, Jessie," I entreat. With my center of gravity destabilized, the quicker we arrive at our destination, the better. "We can go now. Hurry up. There are no cars coming."

"I can't," says Jessie, shrinking back, "Mommy says I can't cross the street unless somebody holds my hand."

A quarter of a century has gone by since my kids were young, but my anxiety has triggered a set of disturbing recollections. I remember this feeling of panic. I remember feeling inadequate in the face of conflicting demands. I remember how often I desperately wished for another pair of hands. I remember that no matter how baffled and frustrated I was, it made absolutely no difference.

This week is teaching me that I'm not one bit more omnipotent or all-knowing than I ever was. Every time I think I have everything under control, reality spits in my face.

After gymnastics, I make it home with both kids. I began to change Danny's poopy diaper. My fingers struggle with the catch on the box of wipes while Danny squirms mightily, and his not-yet-clean bottom messes the terry cloth pad he's lying on, the railings of his changing table, and even the wall. All this happens in thirty seconds.

I remember this feeling of disbelief. I remember viewing with horror the chaos two youngsters could create in just a few minutes. I remember that in some other room in the house my children were always messing at twice the speed I could clean. I remember that feeling overwhelmed and angry altered nothing. I couldn't quit parenthood. Ever.

When my children were little, I couldn't imagine the day after tomorrow — never mind my life after motherhood. It was hard to believe that one day the people at my table would put their food in their mouths and their poops in the toilet.

This deep into winter, children are bored with their toys, numbed by too much TV, and irritable from earaches and endless runny noses. Not only is one of every pair of mittens lost by now, so, I bet, is every young mother's sense of perspective.

Let me reassure you: I promise this stage of parenting is just one brief scene in the movie that is your life. Slowly but surely, you will reclaim your time, your concentration, your sense of yourself as a competent person. Don't give up hope of an uninterrupted conversation, a moment of solitude, a house that doesn't look as if small tornadoes have whirled through one room after another. You will once again take your freedom for granted. One day not too far in the future, I swear, the only one you'll have to read to at bedtime is you.

And if you're lucky, a small event some day, like a granddaughter's mittened hand holding tight to your extended little finger, will reassure you that the seasons of sacrifice you spent caring for your children have touched the course of your life like a blessing.

June 1996

MY GRANDDAUGHTER was making regular appearances in this column by the time she was two. In contrast, I've barely breathed a word about my two-year-old grandson, Danny. I see him all the time. I love him to pieces, but as the mother of two girls, I wasn't adequately prepared to have a boy in my life.

At least, not *this* boy.

I can confess now that at first I thought Danny might be autistic. I kept silent, but here was this baby, home from the hospital a whole week, and he wasn't making eye contact. I remembered the instant connection Jessie and I had made from birth, but Danny stared into space or looked away when I placed myself in his line of sight. I quietly called a pediatrician and received his reassurance that this was normal.

Danny did eventually look at me, but not with the same fervor with which he eyed trucks and trains. When Jessie and I played together, she focused on our interaction. Danny, on the other hand, was totally engrossed in his tasks. Playing in a sandbox, he'd be so focused on sifting and shoveling that I often felt tempted to pick up a book. To Danny, the interpersonal seemed incidental.

I always told Jessie stories while we drove in the car, and she always paid rapt attention. With Danny, as I paused for effect after the wolf said, "I'll huff and I'll puff," he'd shout excitedly, "Truck." Soon all our interactions on the road went like this:

Danny: "Truck."

Nana: "Ooooh, a big truck."

Danny: "Big truck."

This was his idea of a truly fascinating conversation.

I could understand why Danny liked tunnels, and pushing his cars in and out, in and out, of tunnels. I accept that anatomy is destiny, but what is there about large-wheeled vehicles that hooks boys? From my point of view, what is even vaguely interesting?

On our morning together each week, I'd take Danny to watch some nearby construction because I knew he loved it. I'd feel his body come alive with a mixture of fear and delight as he watched backhoes and bulldozers at work and think to myself, *What about this thrills him so much?*

And, *Will I ever be able to empathize?*

This winter, however, something changed. Perhaps it was a natural progression, an inevitable result of his growing older. Perhaps attentive parents and a large and loving extended family socialized it into him. In any case, one day I was pushing a small metal jet onto the runway of his airport. The next moment, he was driving a busload of imaginary people out to meet my plane. I got so excited that we were playing together that I scooped him up and danced him all around the house.

Two days later he met me at the door screaming, "Nana! Nana!"

I can't say whether nature or nurture has made Danny who he is, or whether his task orientation is a facet of his personality or his gender, but learning to share my grandson's interests has been a big stretch for me. I've had to overcome my initial reluctance, then go through the motions of sharing Danny's enthusiasm until I could muster some of my own. My brother lent us his son's Brio train collection, and I'm actually quite proud of the elaborate train layouts I build with Danny every week. And I create awesome obstacle courses for the Matchbox cars that manage to survive their trips around a loop of plastic raceway.

These days Danny and I drive to the train station and tremble when the train roars in. We make roads for trucks in the sandbox and enjoy the sound of Sergeant Murphy's motorcycle on Danny's Golden *Touch 'n' Listen* storybook. I've interested him in digging up worms from my yard and feeding them to my friend Gail's chickens. He lies across a swing, and I twist him around and around until he twirls through the air like a Frisbee.

I get a definite kick out of being with Danny.

Grandchildren, they say, keep you young.

This one's introducing me to my inner boy.

July 1996

THE SOULS OF CHILDREN
are amazing.

Last weekend my husband and I took our grandson, now two-and-a-half, to see the Green Mountain Flyer, a diesel engine that pulls restored 1890s coaches on a twenty-six-mile trip through the green hills of Vermont. We intended to take him for a ride on one of the old passenger cars, but we missed its departure and settled for a visit to the station instead.

Danny is fascinated by trains, probably because his dad takes one to work every day. There's nothing he loves more than to meet his father at the train station; there's nothing he's more afraid of than the thundering noise of the huge locomotive as it shudders to a stop before letting Daddy go. Danny, who loves train books, T-shirts with trains on them, Brio trains, and Thomas the Tank Engine videos, was, to put it mildly, ecstatic about our adventure.

We arrived at the Chester Depot in a pouring rain, and after checking out the building, discovered an old, green caboose sitting on a siding, open for exploration. It was solid and sedate and safe — except to Danny, who wouldn't get within fifty feet of it.

I left my husband and Danny on the grass, entered the train car, peeked out the window, then waved from the platform on the far side. Danny stared out from under his grandfather's umbrella, feet in a puddle, refusing to budge. Then I stood with Danny, holding the umbrella while he watched his grandpa walk up the stairs, enter the car, look out the window, and wave at us. Danny still refused to enter. He also refused to leave. Finally, we all gathered under the umbrella to figure out what to do next.

Danny, usually so brave, was being silly. The caboose, we pointed out, was not hitched to an engine and so could not move. We showed him how the track ended in the mud. We described the nice tables, the soft chairs, the wood stove inside. We agreed Grandpa would carry him if he was scared.

"No," he murmured to all suggestions.

"Let's all go see it together," I said cheerfully, as if we were buddies on the road to Oz, but Danny shook his head, his body as stiff with resistance as a tin man with rusted joints. We could have ended this nonsense, picked Danny up and carried him into the caboose to teach him that his grandparents knew best — there was nothing to be frightened of in a stationary caboose — but we didn't. I think there's something to be said for supporting a child's instinctive caution.

On the one hand, the whole culture disapproves of fearful boys, heaping them with epithets like "scaredy-cat," "sissy," and "baby." On the other hand, with the world such a dangerous place, it's important that children learn to trust themselves in questionable situations. More than anything, our kids need to develop the confidence to rely upon their own intuition rather than give in to pressures from outside. To have overridden Danny's reluctance would have undermined his ability to have faith in his own feelings.

There was another consideration as well: Danny's in awe of trains, enthralled by their size and power. Their very being fills him with fear and wonder. Why be in a rush to take that belief in magic away? What could be gained by convincing Danny that a caboose was nothing more than an ordinary collection of walls and windows and wheels? Would his life be richer if he became aware that there was nothing that exciting in it?

A friend's child recently dismissed a very violent movie by saying, "I wasn't scared. I've seen badder movies lots of times." Cool and jaded at five. Is that an improvement?

I felt, watching Danny, as if I were catching a glimpse of the earliest expression of spirituality in human beings, for what is the basis of religion but the feelings of one small person dazzled by a greater power that both captivates and terrifies? We know that early experiences stimulate the physical development of specific areas of the brain, turning what is mere potential in the newborn into a genuine aptitude in later life. In these few early years, a mind becomes capable of awe only through practice.

When I looked at Danny, his feet firmly set apart, his heart thudding, his eyes filled with a thrilling mixture of excitement and anxiety, I didn't see a "fraidy-cat."

I saw my grandson, the theologian.

The Final Piece of the Puzzle

My daughter Laura and I decided to give a talk on mothering from two perspectives — hers, as the mother of two young children; mine, as the mother of two grown women. In preparation, I asked my friends for advice on how to successfully parent adults.

Everyone gave the same answer: You have to learn to let go.

"You have to give up the role of omnipotent mother," is how one of my friends put it, "and see yourself as just another person doing the best she can." That seemed excellent advice about *what* to do, but I was still left with the question of *how*. How do you give up the conviction that if your kids would only listen to you, they could save themselves from repeating your mistakes?

In my case, it's been a long and continuous process.

I can still remember the night I gave Laura advice about how to handle boys. She turned to me with the compassion only a fourteen-year-old can muster toward a hopelessly out-of-date mother and said, "Mom, things don't work that way anymore."

I nodded because I knew she was right, and from that point on we made the agreement that I'd be a consultant whose advice she could take or ignore. As it worked out, that arrangement actually made it easier for her to listen. She might dismiss one of my suggestions with a frown, but more than a few times I heard her saying to friends on the phone, "You know what my mother thinks . . . ?"

I eventually settled for considering myself what psychologist D.W. Winnicott calls being a "good enough" mother, which feels like high praise in these difficult times. But those words don't reveal the whole truth. Even good enough mothers can be inadequate and hurtful at times. My love for my children may have always been strong and constant, but that didn't keep me from being out of control at times, occasionally stupid, and at one or two critical moments, utterly and absolutely wrong.

It's easy to say I did the best I could. That certainly was the case, but I had to admit to myself that some of the things I'd done had hurt my children, that sometimes just the way I was could be hurtful, and that no matter what excuses I could muster in my own defense, I couldn't undo a thing.

It's tempting to want to protect oneself by glossing over a bad decision, an impulsive act, or even moments of cruelty to one's own flesh and blood. We think if we don't bring it up, it will be forgotten. In truth, only when we bring it up and express our own genuine sorrow and regret, can it be forgiven.

I let Laura down after she slipped a disc in her back just before her graduation from high school. I know now that she tried to protect me from what she was going through during her freshman year at college because she believed I couldn't handle the truth. If I'd been better able to tolerate her pain, I'd also have known she needed to come home.

When Jack had a gall bladder attack and was hospitalized after an operation, I did something equally indefensible to Julie, who was in high school at the time. She wasn't being the most cooperative child in the world and so, as we were driving somewhere, I yelled at her, "Do you think you could try being considerate? My husband is in the hospital."

She yelled back, "Why don't you try being considerate of me? My *father* is in the hospital."

And then, although she'd only said to me exactly what I'd said to her, I stopped the car and threw her out on the street four miles from home on a cold March afternoon. I may have been tired and worried, but I can't excuse my behavior on the grounds that I didn't know how much it would hurt her. My mother once angrily threw me out of the car when I was about the same age, and I still remember the misery of that long, lonely walk home.

It hasn't been easy to relive these bleak moments of my career as a mother, nor to recognize how powerful an impact my behavior has had upon my children. If I could have erased the past, I would have, but instead I decided it was not too late to sit down with each of my daughters and ask her how she experienced those terrible times. I listened. I was truly sorry for what I'd done. I expressed my sincere regrets. And instead of renewing old angers, these conversations allowed us to put the past to rest and start over with a clean slate.

Acknowledging our past mistakes is one of the best ways of keeping ourselves from playing God. Knowing that the person we are is imperfect and often mistaken doesn't stop us from occasionally speaking with the voice of experience, but it makes us much less sure that our advice is exactly what our family needs to hear. It makes us much more tolerant of other people's choices. It allows us to support them without trying to control them.

Facing the truth about ourselves seems to be the key to letting go of those we love.

It is also, I have discovered, the secret to keeping them close.

LINDA WELTNER

Photograph by John Fogle.

Linda Weltner's weekly column "Ever So Humble" has appeared in the *Boston Globe* for sixteen years, is syndicated through The New York Times Wire Service, and has brought her national attention, including being named Best Columnist by the New England Women's Press Association.

As an active member of the New England Speakers' Association, Weltner is a popular public speaker and has spoken at such schools as Harvard Divinity School, Harvard Medical School, Tufts, Wellesley, Brandeis, and Boston College, as well as before more than two hundred sixty women's groups, library audiences, churches, hospital auxiliaries, and charitable organizations throughout New England.

An accomplished author, Weltner's previous books include *No Place Like Home* (1989, Morrow; Quill Paperback), *The New Voice* (1981, Beacon Press), and *Beginning to Feel the Magic* (1981, Little, Brown and Company; Fawcett Juniper Paperback). Weltner is also a contributing editor to *New Age Journal*, and her byline has appeared in such popular magazines as *Woman, New Woman, McCalls, Reader's Digest,* and *Utne Reader.*

Linda Weltner's life experience has taken her from being a graduate of Wellesley College, to being a textbook editor at Little, Brown and Company, and then a teacher in Chelsea, Michigan. A former student at Harvard Divinity School, she has an honorary doctor of letters degree from Regis College. As a mother, she has raised two daughters, Laura and Julie, and is now grandmother to Jessie and Danny. She lives with her husband, Jack, who is a child psychiatrist, and their dog, Pandora, in Marblehead, Massachusetts.